D1573650

Publisher's Review

'Where is the human in migration? In an age of immigration as political posturing and propaganda, Massocki presents a collage of dreams, journeys, tears, wills... even death. This book is an intimate retelling of lives and stories that strips migrants of convenient agenda-driven labels, baring them stark to the reader. With blood running in their veins, vulnerable to fear, driven by ambition—the emotive human is at the centre of Massocki's latest work. *The Pride of an African Migrant* is a frank expository conversation for today and of all time. It is a book that every immigration player should read—from potential migrants to diplomatic staff, immigration officials, foreign policy advisors... every person with a migrant family member or neighbour.'

—**Pierced Rock Press**

The Pride of an African Migrant

Praise for 'The Pride of an African Migrant'

'Mixing politics and philosophy with the personal, Massocki recounts his troubling yet powerful tale of migration from Africa to Europe. His memoir weaves in a rich and unusual variety of voices: from individuals he met along his journey, to those of presidents, philosophers, musicians and academics. The result is a provocative, political memoir that seeks to inform people of the realities of migrating to Europe: a call on Africans to embrace their pride and dignity.'

—**Dr Melanie Griffiths, University of Birmingham, England, UK**

'This is a contemporary mental, physical, and political odyssey. I have not come across such a graphic and personal account of a migrant's extensive experience of former Prime Minister Theresa May's "hostile environment" in all its finery. It is a powerful book. The more I go back to it, the more I see its potential to change minds—those of migrants and even those of people not forced to migrate. I think its publication is very significant.'

—**Bill MacKeith, founder–member of Campaign to Close Campsfield and End All Immigration Detention (also involved with the Bail Observation Project (BOP), National Coalition of Anti-Deportation Campaigns (NCADC) / Right to Remain, Migreurop, Barbed Wire Britain, and Detention Forum)**

'Where else but in the telling of stories of oppression and injustices will one be able to grasp the rawness of avoidable human suffering? No other writer but Massocki Ma Massocki can bring us, in the most gripping way, a story so real that we feel our hairs stand on their ends. We see the gaping horror of what asylum seekers from Africa faced in the UK. Through this book, Massocki is calling for our compassion, asking us to collectively stand up to this scourge of violations to human rights. Massocki believes that we can overcome anything through collective, worldwide efforts in advocating for our rights to dignity.'

—**Dr Toyin Ajao, African Leadership Centre and University of Pretoria**

The Pride of an African Migrant

THE PRIDE OF AN AFRICAN MIGRANT:
In Remembrance of Jimmy Mubenga, a Martyr of Globalisation, Murdered by the UK Border Regime on a British Airways Flight to Angola

Revised Edition

MASSOCKI MA MASSOCKI

Pierced Rock Press

Pierced Rock Press
www.piercedrockpress.com

Copyright ©2020 Massocki Ma Massocki

All rights reserved.

No part of this publication may be reproduced, stored in a retrieval system or transmitted in any form or by any means, electronic, mechanical, photocopying, recording or otherwise, without the prior written permission of the publisher.

Hardcover ISBN: 978-9956-465-04-0
Paperback ISBN: 978-9956-465-05-7
eBook ISBN: 978-9956-465-06-4

Cover by: Kevin Blaire and Bienvenido Junior Swinton
Interior by: Rohit

Pierced Rock Press is a publishing house of Pierced Rock, a conglomeration of numerous companies involved in art and mass media enterprise.

Our mission is to promote human rights in general and the African people's rights in particular and promote African literature.

Thank you for buying an authorised edition of this book. You are sustaining our important work and ensuring that the press achieves its mission.

Pierced Rock Press is committed to publishing works of quality and integrity. In that spirit, we are proud to offer this book to our readers; however, the story, the experiences and the words are the author's alone.

DEDICATION

Above anyone and anything else, I dedicate this book to Jimmy Mubenga, an Angolan asylum seeker killed by the UK border regime at Heathrow Airport on a British Airways flight to Angola on October 12, 2010.

May he be at peace with his ancestors, and his wife and children be strengthened by his memory to truly live on in spite of loss and pain.

The Pride of an African Migrant is also dedicated to migrants of all ages and genders: men, women and children. To travellers seeking bread, home and safety in foreign lands, may you find fulfilment in your journey.

The Pride of an African Migrant

ACKNOWLEDGEMENT

I am grateful to the following people for giving me the support and inspiration that I needed to accomplish this book.

Rachel Luna LLaguno

Rachel Luna LLaguno, one of the most beautiful women I have ever met and my girlfriend, gave me her immeasurable love and support. Without her, this book would not have existed—at least, not now.

Sarah Jane and Her Family

Sarah Jane provided the computer with which I wrote this book, put a roof over my head and clothed and fed me. With her, I learned what love is all about: to think of others over oneself. She encouraged me to write and realised my advocacy and potential even before I did. I am genuinely grateful to her and her lovely daughters, Aisya and Aleha, her mom and dad and the rest of her family.

Roland Musi

Roland Musi, my colleague and good friend, will forever hold a special place in The Pride of an African Migrant. Through his guidance and support, this book paved the way for the birth of the Pierced Rock Foundation (PRF), a nongovernmental organisation (NGO) that aims to reduce the irregular migration of Africans that ends thousands of lives each year.

PRF aims to achieve this by educating Africans on different opportunities for success locally, and the harsh realities of African migrants abroad. The NGO also promotes democracy, human rights and equal opportunity by fighting corruption, nepotism and other ills that alienate African citizens from the system.

Roland is also the founder of LINK-UP, a Cameroonian NGO that provides easier access to quality education and promotes community development and economic empowerment. A survey revealed that only 7% of children in Cameroon could afford textbooks. In response to this issue, LINK-UP provides free textbooks and facilitates scholarships for underprivileged children, especially orphans. The NGO also constructs libraries in villages and remote areas of Cameroon, organises entrepreneurship programmes and provides small-scale capital to businesses. To support Roland and LINK-UP, please visit their website at http://www.linkupchildren.org/.

David Keizan Scott, StoneWater Zen Sangha, Mbeleg Batchom and Carl Swanson

Zen Buddhist teacher David Keizan Scott, StoneWater Zen Sangha, Mbeleg Batchom and Carl Swanson also contributed immensely to this book, for which I am truly grateful.

OUR HEARTS ARE WITH YOU

To the family of our late brother, Jimmy Mubenga:

Widow and orphans, wipe away your tears. Trust that 'God works in mysterious ways'. Your husband and father died so others could live and be awakened.

Jimmy fought and died so that we can all have the right to live with our families, spouses and children. He will be remembered for his protection of kunde: our human rights. Jimmy is truly a martyr of globalisation.

Jimmy has become immortal and can never die. He would live in our memories and stories, empowering black communities and inspiring those who seek justice and freedom.

May you be strengthened by his memory to truly live on in spite of loss and pain.

The world remembers Jimmy Mubenga.

The Pride of an African Migrant

AUTHOR'S NOTE

The Pride of an African Migrant is my first book. All the events described have happened as I remember or as I was told.

This is a revised edition. The first edition, which was scheduled to be published on May 4, 2020, was not published because of the COVID-19 outbreak. However, promotional copies have already been distributed three months prior to publication.

The first edition received several corrections, suggestions, questions and critiques, which I humbly welcomed. Given this, I have written this new edition to address all misunderstandings from the first edition. Every chapter has been scrutinized, and several new chapters have been added.

This revised edition is final.
www.massockimamassocki.com

The Pride of an African Migrant

TABLE OF CONTENTS

FOREWORD xvii

PREFACE TO THE REVISED EDITION xxi

INTRODUCTION 1

PART 1: COLONISATION 7
1 The Colonial Psychological Legacy 9

PART 2: BAD GOVERNANCE AND
NEOCOLONISATION 17
2 Revolution Now 19

PART 3: THE JOURNEY TO PARADISE 31
3 From Cameroon to England 33

PART 4: PARADISE LOST 41
4 The Street Life and the Colorisation of Fear 43
5 Hope Again 49
6 Trapped by a Gangster 53
7 A Shadow Of Happiness 61

PART 5: HUMAN RIGHTS 63
8 Seeking Asylum 65
9 International Refugee Week 77
10 Jimmy Mubenga: A Martyr of Globalisation 81
11 Fleeing from Liverpool 89

PART 6: SOUL'S JOURNEY 95
12 Sarah Jane 97
13 Returning to Liverpool 107

PART 7: PRIDE AND DIGNITY 119
14 Returning Home 121
15 Let Us Keep Our Pride and Dignity 137
16 We Can Achieve Our Dreams While Being In Africa 143
17 Escapism Is Not the Solution 151

PART 8: GLOBALISATION 155
18 Global Village 157
19 Pros and Cons of Immigration 159

PART 9: DEVELOPMENT 163
20 Rethinking Development 165

PART 10: DENOUEMENT 171
21 We Are One 173

FOREWORD

Let me begin by emphasising the fact that travelling is the highest school of learning. The benefits that come with exposure to education, the skills migrants bring back when they return to their home countries and the remittances for those who prefer to stay and work abroad cannot be overlooked.

Despite the challenging immigration laws, did you know that there are more black immigrants from Africa with a college degree than any other immigrant group in the US? According to the US census data, Nigerian immigrants have the highest level of education in the nation, surpassing whites and Asians. In Philosophy and Opinions of Marcus Garvey: Africa for the Africans, Marcus Garvey, the Pan-African leader, is quoted as saying, 'Education is the medium by which a people are prepared for the creation of their own particular civilization, and the advancement and glory of their own race'. In other words, the purpose of education is to prepare people to solve the problems of their own societies.

The black world suffers from a severe brain drain because the most educated among us are often busy solving other people's problems. If the spirit that drives black people to achieve the highest level of academic success was harnessed for the benefit of our people, imagine how much progress could be made.

Illegally travelling or living in another country when your visa has already expired is always a crime under international law. Hence, migrants who have overstayed their visas or do not have the necessary papers often become highly vulnerable and exposed to forced deportation, as well as other forms of humiliation. Africans, in particular, are not informed of the immigration system in the EU. The lack of information leaves them trapped in situations that are worse than they could have ever imagined.

I am not out to expose the wickedness or human rights abuses in the handling of the matter concerning migrants. This has already been handled well by the personal experiences of Massocki (the author) and the experiences of other African migrants mentioned in this book. I assume these abuses were—and are—carried out to deter other migrants from visiting these countries. However, many potential migrants are unaware of this before embarking on their journeys. Thus, a book like this is necessary to help Africans understand such issues so that they can be better prepared before starting their own journey.

One fact is obvious: over 90% of African migrants travel for business, education or economic reasons. Less than 10% travel as refugees. However, many often concoct stories of this nature and present themselves to asylum centres with hopes of obtaining papers that would allow them to live in these countries as refugees. This method of regularising one's stay in Europe and other developed countries used to be easy, but today, most Western governments have recognised this approach. To discourage informal migrants from using this method, the process of handling asylum applications has been unreasonably slowed down, with some files taking more than 10 to 15 years to get processed. In some countries, asylum centres are located on islands like Lampedusa in Italy or the Canary Islands in Spain—areas with little to no economic activity that would keep the migrants active.

The Pride of an African Migrant

This brilliant work of Massocki is imperative for my African brothers and sisters. In particular, this book will help them understand this fact and prevent them from following unfounded dreams of travelling to Europe without the capacity to properly integrate themselves in these countries and reap the benefits that may follow.

Thanks to the Internet, knowledge has been decentralised and brought to our doorsteps for those eager to learn. You can now learn in Africa and still compete for the best jobs anywhere in the world and travel as a consultant or an expatriate. However, most migrants moving into these countries for work neither have the necessary skills, nor are able to speak other languages. This makes integration a long and challenging process, subsequently promoting the development of ghetto communities with thousands of undocumented migrants carrying the image of unwanted guests to the citizens and governments of other countries.

One fact that most Africans on the continent do not understand is that less than 5% of African migrants in the EU are successful. Those who are successful are also confronted with another problem: racism. Westerners have often portrayed themselves as superior human beings as compared to other races. Immigrants and blacks, in particular, are most often reminded of this.

There are many examples of racism. Let me describe them to you by citing a few cases that happened recently at the time of writing: a black Barcelonian football player was thrown a banana while the game was ongoing. This was to remind him that even though he was playing very well, he was still considered a monkey. He picked up the banana, ate part of it and threw away the rest. A similar incident is the case of a wealthy basketball team owner who was overheard telling his mistress that he would not like to have black people watch basketball matches. This created a huge reaction from all sectors of the American society—from President Barack Obama to the basketball league president. In the end, the team owner was asked to pay a fine of millions of dollars and was banned from participating in any activity related to the game.

This is just the tip of the iceberg of the frustration successful Africans face abroad. Minor cases of racism take place at various job sites; each day, our fellow brothers and sisters are reminded of the fact that they do not belong to that community. Meanwhile, in Africa, these Westerners are treated like demigods.

Massocki's story is a rare, personal account detailing the challenges involved in being integrated into the EU, his realisation that pursuing papers in Europe is like chasing the wind and his eventual decision to voluntarily return to his beautiful country of Cameroon. This book is more than a straightforward narrative. It is my wish for other migrants trapped in similar situations to be courageous enough to make this tough decision. I hope families would be supportive and welcome these migrants similar as to how the 'prodigal son was welcomed by his father' in the Bible.

Other Africans aspiring to migrate to the EU or the US should understand these issues and be better prepared before embarking on their trip outside Africa.

ROLAND MUSI
Founder and President of LINK-UP Development Group

PREFACE TO THE REVISED EDITION

Most people are confused about the distinction among refugees, asylum seekers and migrants. However, under the United Nations High Commissioner for Refugees (UNHCR), these cases are different. In particular, refugees have no choice but to seek refuge in another country for reasons such as violence or persecution, while asylum seekers apply to take refuge in another country out of the fear of persecution. Consequently, not all asylum seekers will be registered as refugees. On the other hand, migrants voluntarily move to a different country because of their countries' economic situations. Although they are different, all of them experience new environments, new cultures and new sets of laws, which may either be in their favour or not.

This book examines the treatment of African migrants in the Western world. Furthermore, an analysis of factors, such as colonization and race, that have contributed to human rights violations against Africans and a discussion of Jimmy Mubenga's case reveal how the justice system is flawed, especially for African migrants. Ultimately, the book raises the following main question: Are the established human rights only meant to benefit a certain race?

As a continent, Africa suffers from mental colonialism, which is seen in how African migrants choose to stay in detention centres rather than return to Africa. We believe other continents are better than ours, but we have to remember that African countries are young and have been colonized, a fate that continues to haunt us today. However, to achieve the continent that we dream of, we need to invest, work and hold our leaders accountable. For this endeavour, The Pride of an

African Migrant serves as a guide in achieving a stable continent.

Deraso Dokhlohe is the ambassadress of the African Capitals of Culture in East Africa and the founder of 'A Day As A Refugee', which is a nongovernmental organization aiming to examine the living standards of every refugee, conduct research and formulate solutions for the refugee crisis.

INTRODUCTION

The Pride of an African Migrant narrates my life as a young Cameroonian in the United Kingdom. It is the memoir of an African migrant that provides a lens to the panorama of the lives of African migrants in Europe, particularly that of African asylum seekers in the UK.

I travelled to England to pursue higher education. However, financial constraints hindered me from completing my studies, and I ended up as an irregular immigrant. In the hope of continuing my studies, I sought asylum in the UK, which was later denied to me. I eventually became a destitute asylum seeker, which gave me the chance to witness the life of other asylum seekers, especially African asylum seekers. Their lives, I found, are characterised by homelessness, hunger, torture, imprisonment, assassinations, suicide and many more.

The Western world claims to be the model and pinnacle of human rights and democracy in the world. In the name of these principles, they invade other nations and kill hundreds of thousands of innocent men, women and children. They cause suffering to millions with the inhabitants of their own countries subject to indescribable violations of human rights. This is the case in the UK where asylum seekers, in general, and African asylum seekers, in particular, are victims of grave acts of torture and assassination, regardless of the 1951 Refugee Convention of the United Nations High Commissioner for Refugees (UNHCR).

This raises the question: Are human rights and democracy just other pretexts used by Western powers to fulfil their colonialist ambitions? This argument stems from the reality that such authorities do not respect the basic human rights of those residing in their own countries.

The UK is not only a simple state member of the United Nations. It is also one of its five permanent Security Council members. These five members, especially the UK, should know by heart the United Nations' Universal Declaration of Human Rights better than any other state member. In Article 14, the Universal Declaration of Human Rights says:

> *'Everyone has the right to seek and to enjoy in other countries asylum from persecution.'*

And in its preamble, it is written:

> *'Whereas recognition of the inherent dignity and the equal and inalienable rights of all members of the human family is the foundation of freedom, justice and peace in the world.'*

It is worth reemphasising that in the UK, asylum seekers who voluntarily refuse to return to their countries, mainly Africans, are subjected to extreme violations of human rights, torture, imprisonment, assassinations and forced deportations by the UK border regime, regardless of the principle of non-refoulment contained in Article 33 of the 1951 Refugee Convention—with the UK as the signatory.

> *No Contracting State shall expel or return ('refouler') a refugee in any manner whatsoever to the frontiers of territories where his life or freedom would be threatened*

The Pride of an African Migrant

on account of his race, religion, nationality, membership of a particular social group or political opinion.

Without violating the state's sovereign right to determine who enters and stays in their territory, on September 19, 2016, the United Nations General Assembly unanimously adopted the New York Declaration for Refugees and Migrants, which reaffirms the dignity and human rights of people on the move regardless of their migratory status.

For resisting his deportation in 2010, Jimmy Mubenga, an African asylum seeker, was tortured and killed at Heathrow Airport by the UK border regime.

Having peacefully protested against the killing of Mubenga, I was arrested and detained naked in a freezing cell. After some time, even the place I was staying at was set on fire, ready to kill me. This book is an appeal to the UNHCR and the UN High Commissioner for Human Rights (UNHCHR) for them to look at these matters properly and identify appropriate measures.

John J. Mearsheimer said:

'The most powerful states in the system create and shape institutions so that they can maintain their share of world power or even increase it'.

However, I still believe in these institutions, despite the direct participation of United Nations' Peacekeepers in the overthrow and assassination of DR Congo's Prime Minister, Patrice Lumumba, in 1961, and the slaughtering of Tutsis by Hutu on the first day of the Rwandan genocide at a school where 90 UN troops armed with a machine gun were planted at the entrance of the school.

In their published article 'The Death of Jimmy Mubenga: How the UK's Legal System Cast a Black Man beyond Justice', the magazine New Humanist wrote:

> In the case of Mubenga, his death presents a paradox. First, an inquest jury concluded that he was held down by one or more of the guards. The following year, an Old Bailey jury reached a not-guilty verdict for all three guards, leaving open the possibility that Mubenga held himself down. But according to Dr Fegan-Earl, the forensic pathologist, that is improbable because our 'inner self-preserving mechanisms' mean the body would instinctively try to escape that position. So, should we accept that Jimmy Mubenga's death is an unaccountable mystery? Or should we see it as evidence of the possibility that the deportee in Britain today, like the unarmed black male citizen of the United States, is so deprived of rights that acts committed against them are no longer crimes?
>
> I can't breathe. An inherently distressing phrase, but after the deaths of Eric Garner last summer in New York and Jimmy Mubenga in 2010 at London's Heathrow airport, this short sentence has come to embody something more sinister. I can't breathe. Two men on two different continents, both heard speaking these words minutes before they died. Two men in two liberal democracies, both being physically restrained by officers on behalf of the state. In both cases, the officers did not perform the standard first-aid resuscitation technique because, they said, they thought the men were still

breathing. In both cases, the men who died were unarmed. They were both black, in their forties, and married with children. I can't breathe. These three words seem to capture the reality of racism and justice in the US and the UK.

Some might say there is less injustice in this country. Eventually, the three G4S detainee custody officers who were restraining 46-year-old Mubenga on board a plane shortly before he died were charged with manslaughter. They underwent a criminal trial at the Old Bailey. They were all acquitted, yes, but not before they had been cross-examined in a court of law. Not so in Garner's case. Despite autopsy findings that the 43-year-old died from a chokehold and the compression of his chest, no charge was brought against any officer.

Racist texts found on the mobile phones of the officers who killed Mubenga coupled with the recent Brexit reveal that the xenophobic sentiment is still too strong in the UK for British people to let go of. Such sentiments are fuelled by politicians in the name of patriotism, indistinguishable from xenophobia. Therefore, it is high time for international organisations to take action against both politicians with xenophobic rhetoric and political parties with a xenophobic social program.

The well-known ancient Chinese philosopher Lao Tzu said: 'When the country falls into chaos, patriotism is born.' We can paraphrase Lao Tzu and say: When the UK falls into chaos, Brexit is born.

The Brexit is a red line that has been crossed. UK's membership in the EU was an anti-xenophobic training ground for British people; with the Brexit, all hopes of multiculturalism and tolerance have disappeared. The Brexit simply means that the British people do not want Europeans in their country. They do not even want their fellow white people in their country. What does this leave African asylum seekers and immigrants in the UK, not to mention the thousands who are on their way to the country? Are they not going to suffer the fate of Mubenga? Are they not future martyrs of globalisation who will be sacrificed on the altar of British nationalism?

By outlining barbaric acts of torture to which African asylum seekers are being subjected in the UK, I aim to remind the UK of the present situation so that they would strive to attain what they claim to be an ideal practice of human rights—a harmonious state of coexistence. Moreover, this is a call upon organisations such as the UNHCR and the UNHCHR to provide accurate assessments of how countries treat their inhabitants and perform their job, which is to protect human rights.

I interviewed some African asylum seekers who were victims of grave acts of torture in the UK, and I narrate here their shocking and unbelievable stories. This memoir aims to fight xenophobia and promote harmonious coexistence between all human beings, between migrants and Europeans in particular, as well as heighten people's compassion and wisdom, which are imperative for world peace. The book's goal is also to inform Africans aspiring to migrate to the European Union or the US of the issues related to their plans so that they can be better prepared.

PART 1:

COLONISATION

The Pride of an African Migrant

1
THE COLONIAL PSYCHOLOGICAL LEGACY

'Without subscribing to the view that Africa gained nothing at all in her long encounter with Europe, one could still say, in all fairness, that she suffered many terrible and lasting misfortunes. In terms of human dignity and human relations, the encounter was almost a complete disaster for the black race. It has warped the mental attitudes of both black and white.'

—Chinua Achebe, The Black Writer's Burden

European magazines, series, movies and television programmes populate African public spaces, with some being highly popular content around the world. These media present Europe as an El Dorado: a land filled with opportunity, fantasy and adventure of which the local African can only dream. Pitched against poor living conditions and a colonial psychological legacy of white superiority, they create an almost desperate quest for the white man's land. This culminates in a mass exodus of Africans seeking fulfilment, abandoning all the good things of their land and perpetuating psychological bondage of inferiority, their dreams lost to the endemic of innumerable, undocumented lives snatched by the

Mediterranean and the Sahara. Thousands of Africans lose their lives every year in the desert and the sea just to enter Europe—a land they believe to be an El Dorado.

Luckily, the Nigerian film industry Nollywood, grew to prominence when alternative media representation was most needed to decolonise Africans from overexposure to Western movies that do not reflect the African reality, have no ethnic importance and are morally decadent vis-à-vis the African culture. However, with the onset of the industry's production of Western-style movies that sometimes display disrespect, African culture and values have become less and less capital to Nollywood. For example, Nollywood movies now often degrade the African spiritual tradition by depicting it as evil. This is unlike Hollywood: the single largest export industry of the US into which billions of dollars are poured every year to show the world a pleasant yet fake image of the American society.

Imports like magazines, movies and series are central to Western propaganda as they create the illusion that fools Africans every day. This subtle form of colonialism known as neocolonialism unreservedly preaches that Africans are subhuman and nothing good can come out of Africa.

It is in thinking where people get the idea that being slaves in the Western world is better than being free in Africa. An inherited legacy reinforced by media is a huge contributor to why undocumented African migrants prefer to sleep on the cold streets of Europe and experience various types of suffering rather than return home.

To have a chance to stay in the UK legally, African migrants lucky enough not to be subjected to torture, inflict upon themselves an indescribable and intolerable degree of pain—some would press a scalding iron against their bodies, while others would prefer imprisonment or even commit suicide. Despite this, thousands of Africans still choose to risk their lives every day to cross the dreadful sea to enter Europe. They are willing to go to such great lengths just to avoid returning to Africa.

I met an African asylum seeker named Thierry, who inflicted pain upon himself to receive refugee status in the UK. He voluntarily asked his friends to tie him up and press a scalding iron against his back. After being burnt as if coming from hell, Thierry presented himself to the immigration office and told them that soldiers of his country burned him because he was gay.

One of the most famous cases is that of a Senegalese asylum seeker. Upon being told that he would be deported, he committed suicide in a detention centre. He reasoned that if he killed himself, at least his son would get to remain in the UK.

Another notable case is that of a female Nigerian asylum seeker in England who chose to live in a nursing home with deranged people than return to her country. While being deported back to her homeland, this woman defecated on purpose at the airport and then ate her excrement in front of everyone. She acted as if she were deranged, and everyone believed her. After the incident, she was taken to a nursing home and given medicine for people with mental illness, which affected her own health.

The Pride of an African Migrant

An African migrant who was rescued in the coasts of Italy after the boat he was in sank, killing many of his comrades, said: 'If I were to be sent back to Africa, I would come back again regardless of the risks in the sea. Because Africa is hell, and Europe is paradise'.

When Europeans invaded Africa, they made Africans suffer through forced labour. At the time, the feet of Europeans were never allowed to touch the ground; they never walked on foot and had to be carried around by able-bodied Africans. To maintain their supremacy, Europeans presented themselves as immortals and the incarnation of God on earth. Is it not normal for people who have been subjugated like Africans to strive to seek the land of immortals in the hope that one day, they, too, will become one of them?

In his exile in London, General Charles de Gaulle delivered through the BBC his famous 'We have lost the battle but not the war' speech. At that moment, he called for colonies, especially those in Africa, to come and help liberate Europe from Germany. It was only when Africans were implored to go and save Europe from Germany during World War II that most of them realised that Europeans were not immortals. Not only were most Africans unaware that Europeans were mortals; they also did not know that Europeans defecate just like them—and that Europeans' excrements are even fouler than those of Africans. Here is a story of a young African encapsulating the ill display of neither pride nor dignity.

Once upon a time, there was a young African. After the death of his father, he sold all his inheritance and travelled to Europe just to go and see the excrement of a white man. When he arrived in Europe, he saw excrements everywhere as Europeans did not know toilets. In every street, there were excrements. He stood by the side of the road to see if these excrements are for white men. To his greatest amazement, there were white people defecating everywhere. Seeing this, he told himself, 'We are all the same; they are not greater than us. I defecate, and they defecate too. I am going back to the land of my fathers'. However, the young man had no money left to return to the land of his fathers. He decided to walk from Europe to Africa, but he never arrived. He died in the desert.

I hope our rescued African migrant from the Italian coasts who said 'Africa is hell, and Europe is paradise' will not suffer the same fate as the young African in the story. If this rescued African migrant is allowed to seek asylum in Italy, I wish him good luck. If he thinks that he was lucky to survive the dreadful sea, he will have to be more fortunate to survive the dreadful land of Europe. The Rastafarians call this land Babylon. This rescued migrant will have to be luckier to have accommodation, a job and a residence permit and live legally in Europe, which he considers paradise. What he does not know is that many African migrants, just like him, after many years in Europe, were deprived of these basic needs essential for human survival in the modern world.

However, if Africans have to be lucky or wait for more than a decade to gain access to all these basic needs in Europe, then it would merely be an illusion for them to consider Europe as paradise.

The Pride of an African Migrant

Unknown to our rescued migrant, homelessness, hunger, detention, assassinations, torture and suicide are most probably what await most African migrants on their move to Europe. African migrants are as lucky to avoid all these; for many people, it is like finding a needle in a haystack.

Every year, the terrifying Mediterranean Sea claims the lives of at least 5,000 African migrants. And those who have conquered the sea still have to survive, in the land of Europe, the barbarism and inhumanity of immigration officers. For African migrants, the Mediterranean Sea and the land of Europe are equally dreadful. It goes without saying that for African migrants, reaching Europe is a natural selection—the survival of the fittest. Once in Europe, migrants will see their humanity denied. They will lose the right to education, housing and employment. They will be jailed for months and even years in prison-like detention centres, tortured and forcefully deported back to their countries or worse, killed. All these have made African migrants the martyrs of globalisation.

This massive exodus of Africans is a repeat of our tragic past, reviving in our memories the crack of the whip, the roar of the waves and the clanking of shackles. A 2018 CNN documentary shows migrants from sub-Saharan Africa wanting to enter Europe being held captives, auctioned and subjected to slavery.

In Manila, the capital city of the Philippines, a wealthy Chinese businessman once asked me, 'Is it true that white people went to Africa, stole Africans and enslaved them for many centuries in America?' 'Yes, it is true', was my reply. Then, he asked: 'Why do Africans keep going to the land of their enslavers'?

The Pride of an African Migrant

Why are Africans going to Europe? Why are Asians going to Europe? Why are Latin Americans going to Europe? It is because Europe colonised those peoples. Europe stole the material and human resources of Africa, Asia and Latin America—oil, minerals, uranium, gold and diamonds, even fruits, vegetables, livestock and the people themselves—and used them. Now, new generations of Asians, Latin Americans and Africans are seeking to reclaim that stolen wealth, as they have the right to do.

At the Libyan border, I recently stopped 1,000 African migrants headed for Europe. I asked them why they were going there. They told me it was to take back their stolen wealth—that they would not be leaving otherwise. Who can restore the wealth that was taken from us? If you decide to restore all of this wealth, there will be no more immigration from the Philippines, Latin America, Mauritius and India. Let us have the wealth that was stolen from us. Africa deserves USD 777 trillion in compensation from the countries that colonized it. Africans will demand that amount, and if you do not give it to them, they will go to where you have hidden away those trillions of dollars. They have the right to do so. They have to follow that money and bring it back.

—Muammar Gaddafi in his speech at the 64th General Assembly of the United Nations

The Pride of an African Migrant

PART 2:
BAD GOVERNANCE AND NEOCOLONISATION

The Pride of an African Migrant

2
REVOLUTION NOW

Lord bless Africa
May her glory be lifted high
Hear our petitions
Lord bless us, your children
Lord we ask you to protect our nation
Intervene and end all conflicts
Protect us, protect our nation
Protect...Africa
—The national anthem of South Africa

My stay in the UK not only allowed me to demystify and destroy the European myth; most importantly, it allowed me to understand that for the young African, fighting for social justice should be imperative. It is the only way to prevent the young African from dying in the desert or drowning in the Mediterranean Sea, experiencing the same humiliation and torture suffered by African migrants in Europe. Either through protest movements for social change, we brave the dangerous streets of our dictatorial and terrorist states, or as cowards, we abdicate and accept death in the Mediterranean Sea, suffer the humiliations and tortures reserved to African migrants in Europe.

This is why since my return from the UK, I have committed myself to fighting—by any means necessary—the Cameroonian dictatorial and terrorist regime of President Paul Biya, a regime responsible for the death of thousands of Cameroonians in the desert and the Mediterranean Sea.

Leaders like Biya are what human rights activist and musician Fela Kuti described as 'beasts of no nation, animals in human skin, animals that wear a suit and tie'. From this view, Fela thus declared 'war upon them'.

If leaders like Biya were human beings, they would have known what human rights are. They would have known that humans need food and water, housing, health care and education—luxuries that they are not ready to offer to their populations. African despots not only sit and watch their fellow Africans drowning in the Mediterranean Sea; they also push them to the sea. Either we leave power in the hands of beasts like Biya and die in the Mediterranean Sea and others suffer the fate of Jimmy Mubenga, or we overthrow these beasts using every means necessary. There is no other way around.

A group of African migrants composed a song called 'The Song of the Traveller', which narrates their journey from Africa to Ceuta in Spain, passing through the Sahara—the world's largest desert, a passage that they describe as a ride to hell—and their crossing of the Mediterranean Sea, which claims the lives of at least 5,000 African migrants every year.

In the song, African migrants not only describe the adversities they encountered in their voyage—that will not fail to make you shed tears—but also evoke misery as the primary cause of their migration. The song is thus a call upon their governments to take action against that misery.

The writers of the song also describe how, at one of Spain's borders, they climbed fences that were erected to prevent migrants like them from entering Europe. For them, these fences that continuously tower over them are the least of their concerns as they brave forces of nature—the hellish heat of the Sahara and dreadful waves and storms of the Mediterranean Sea.

Listening to 'The Song of the Traveller', we realise that if we eradicate misery in countries wherein migration has become rampant—sub-Saharan countries, for example—is what will erect a barrier that migrants will never be able to jump.

Furthermore, this song gives us a profound definition of migration: 'a revolt against misery'. This definition is far beyond what international organisations have simply called as 'crossing borders'.

African countries, black sub-Saharan people
Look at your children, who live in poverty
Some of them revolt and say they are volunteers
Volunteers of migration, they go to hustle
They will come back to help you
It is those volunteers who are called travellers
Travellers, pray for travellers
Respect travellers, pray for travellers
We are the travellers, pray for travellers
Travellers in Niger swim in the dust
They live in the heat

The Pride of an African Migrant

They cross the desert; it is a ride to hell
They sleep in yotis
Travellers arrive in war zones
In war zones, they have to sleep in hiding places
Travellers discover the Maghreb
Travellers in Morocco lose their mind
Travellers in Damascus sleep in bushes
Sometimes, when it is winter, it produces heat
Today travellers celebrate the good weather
It's a Friday we left Morocco
Walking in the night, we climbed mountains
We climbed fences; we swam the sea
Today, as we speak to you, we are in Ceuta in Spain
Travellers in Europe, we live the reality
Here in Ceuta, we all live in CETI, the Temporary
Holding Centre for Immigrants

—The Song of the Traveller

Through bad governance, African leaders echo the racist colonial narrative by making young Africans believe that being African is a curse. True enough, they have succeeded in getting Africans to escape from their continent. For many Africans, Africa is just an option. They are still in Africa because they have not yet found the opportunity to go elsewhere. They only remain in Africa because they have no choice, with people preferring to die in the desert and the sea than to stay in their homeland.

Africans go to Europe to seek a better life—something that has been denied to them in their own countries by their leaders. Despite being the wealthiest continent, its residents remain the poorest because of poor governance and neocolonialism.

Democracy, respect for human rights, rule of justice and equal opportunities for all, regardless of whatsoever, are the solutions to this African exodus.

African leaders are not even willing to guarantee basic needs—potable drinking water, electricity, health care and basic education—to their people. In this world, brimming with boundless resources, poverty and misery are violence. These problems are made by humans and have become political tools of oppression and repression for African tyrants in connivance with Western imperialist powers. They destroy the lives of millions of Africans, leaving migration as their only option to survive. Therefore, our definition of a refugee should also include economic migrants as they run away from structural violence.

The sea is dreadful, and for people to embark on such a journey, there must be terror in the land. Yet, nobody acknowledges the terror—at least the economic terror those 'economic migrants' are running away from. Because there are bureaucrats thousands of miles away with the power to decide those who are refugees and those who are not. African despots voluntarily keep systemic poverty flowing in the land to control their citizens and stay in power. Through so-called international institutions and multinationals, Western powers financially terrorise African nations, causing deaths to millions of Africans. To limit violence on a physical level is to misunderstand it. In Defining Violence—Defining Peace, the State University of New York (SUNY) Press, Albany wrote:

> *'When conceptualizing violence, it is important to incorporate all aspects of violence while allowing room for understanding the relationship between the forms. A*

broader paradigm is required—one that includes not just war, torture, homicide and other physical abuse but also emotional abuse, oppression and exploitation.'

In an open letter I addressed to Paul Biya, the Cameroonian dictator, I made him aware that famine and cholera, brought about by unclean drinking water, are deadlier in the far northern region of Cameroon than the Islamic terrorist sect Boko Haram.

'Famine has reached an intolerable level in several villages in the Far North region of Cameroon. Villages where alarming signs of misery and poverty [exist], indicate that it is urgent for measures to be taken in the short- and long-term to solve this alimentary insecurity... Sensible to this situation... the network fighting against hunger (RELUFA) accompanied by journalists on the 7th of June 2013 went down there [to give a voice to populations that suffer alimentary insecurity in the North, more particularly in the far North. Because the press is better placed to forward the information and touch people that can help], said Sandrine Bikele from RELUFA... Populations that can't offer themselves the luxury of education are hit with other problems such as the lack of potable water with diarrhoeas and dysentery as a bonus. In the village of Bozo Ka'e for instance, the nearest medical centre is 5 kilometres away in Douroum; another one is 10 kilometres away in Kallia and the third one is 35 kilometres away in Maroua... [Go and tell Yaoundé, that we women, we need pounding machine and water,' said the spokesperson of the women of Bozo Ka'e]

—Ericien Pascal Nguiamba, Youndéinfo.com

The Pride of an African Migrant

The oppression of Africans by their own leaders in connivance with Western imperialist powers is the major cause of the massive exodus of Africans to the Western world. Simon Kimbagu had prophesied:

> *'The years that will follow the false independence that most African countries will acquire in 1960 will be characterised by a massive exodus of young Africans to the Western world to escape from misery and oppression, which will be caused by African dictators who will take power to serve their own interests and those of Western countries.'*

Swiss multinational Nestlé unfairly competed in the dairy market against Cameroonian dairy company, Codilait, by selling at low prices and selling imitation cow's milk. The incident led to the closure of Codilait, which directly employed 200 Cameroonians in a country where social assistance is a myth. Moreover, each employee of Codilait supported at least 10 family members—a total of 2,000 Cameroonian lives destroyed by Nestlé.

Codilait lodged a lawsuit against Nestlé for unfair competition and fraud, and an independent commission determined that what the foreign company was passing off as cow's milk was not cow's milk at all. While the trial was on-going, Cameroonian dictator Paul Biya met with Nestlé's CEO, and we know the tragic end: despite substantial evidence, Codilait did not receive compensation. Codilait never opened its doors again. Such conspiracy at the highest state level sent 200 Cameroonian citizens to unemployment—in a country where there is no social assistance.

The Pride of an African Migrant

Codilait was located just 100 metres away from Nyalla's Government Secondary School that I attended. The older brother of one of my classmates, a Codilait employee, was the one supporting his education. As soon as the company closed its doors, my classmate also had to stop school. He never went back. The last time I heard from him through Facebook, he said that he left Cameroon and is in Niger on his way to Europe. He might arrive in Europe and, perhaps, in Switzerland. Western multinationals destroy the lives of millions of Africans, leaving migration as their only option to survive. However, the sad reality is that we all know the fate of African migrants in Europe: Homelessness, hunger, torture, imprisonment, assassinations, suicide and many more.

According to a German newspaper, 'through the CFA Franc, France collects EUR 440 billion each year from African countries'.

> *'Fourteen African countries are still obliged to store about 85% of their foreign exchange reserves at the Banque de France in Paris. They are under the direct control of the French Treasury. The countries concerned do not have access to this part of their reserves. As 15% of reserves are insufficient for their needs, they must borrow additional funds from the French Treasury at market prices. Since 1961, Paris controls all foreign exchange reserves in Benin, Burkina Faso, Guinea-Bissau, Côte d'Ivoire, Mali, Niger, Senegal, Togo, Cameroon, Central African Republic, Chad, Congo, Equatorial Guinea and Gabon. In addition, these countries must, each year, transfer their 'colonial debt' for infrastructure built in France to Paris as Silicon Africa 3 reported in detail.'*

—Mathew Ogunsina, Ethiomedia.com

The Pride of an African Migrant

Some African heads of states who dared to denounce or question agreements signed with France were overthrown and even killed by coup d'états financed and organized by France. This was the case for Sylvanus Olympio, Thomas Sankara, Fulbert Youlou, Alphonse Massamba-Débat, Marien Ngouabi, Pascal Lissouba, Barthélémy Boganda and François Tombalbaye, to name a few.

From the nominal independence of most African countries in 1960–2013, France has militarily intervened at least 53 times in Africa.

'In Africa, coup d'états constitute a mode of political regulation, and the real initiators of these coup d'états are Western imperialist states. At the top list of these Western mentors of coup d'état is undeniably France, which has abused its criminal means in its ex colonies in order to maintain its influence... Six out of 10 coup d'états that occurred in the past 60 years in Africa concerned French-speaking countries, particularly sub-Saharan countries within the sphere of influence of 'FrancAfrique'. But almost all these countries signed a military agreement with France; several among them host French military bases that are supposed to protect these countries from armed attacks. Thus, these installations reveal their real function of the maker of political violence in Africa, hidden under secret defence agreements.'

—*Afriqueindependence.wordpress.com*

In his article 'Africa Is Not Poor, We Are Stealing Its Wealth' and published by Al Jazeera, Nick Dearden, director of the UK campaigning organisation, Global Justice Now, writes:

'That's the essence of a report from several campaign groups released today. Based on a set of new figures, it finds that sub-Saharan Africa is a net creditor to the rest of the world, to the tune of more than USD 41 billion. Sure, there's money going in: around USD 161 billion a year in the form of loans, remittances (those working outside Africa and sending money back home) and aid. But there's also USD 203 billion leaving the continent. Some of this is direct, such as USD 68 billion in mainly dodged taxes. Essentially, multinational corporations 'steal' much of this—legally—by pretending they are really generating their wealth in tax havens. These so-called 'illicit financial flows' amount to around 6.1 per cent of the continent's entire gross domestic product (GDP)—or three times what Africa receives in aid. Then there's the USD 30 billion that these corporations 'repatriate'—profits they make in Africa but send back to their home country, or elsewhere, to enjoy their wealth. **The City of London is awash with profits extracted from the land and labour of Africa.** There are also more indirect means by which we pull wealth out of Africa. Today's report estimates that USD 29 billion a year is being stolen from Africa in illegal logging, fishing and trade in wildlife. USD 36 billion is owed to Africa as a result of the damage that climate change will cause to their societies and economies as they are unable to use fossil fuels to develop in the way that Europe did. Our climate crisis was not caused by Africa, but Africans will feel the effect more than most others. Needless to say, the funds are not currently forthcoming. In fact, even this assessment is enormously generous, because it assumes that all of the wealth flowing into Africa is benefitting the people of that continent.'

The Pride of an African Migrant

In his book, 'Cameroon: The Haunted Heart of Africa', Janvier Tchouteu, asks:

> *What is the way forward in dismantling the anachronistic system managed in Cameroon by the puppets of France's political mafia in Africa called FrancAfrique, a political establishment of marionettes of foreign interests acting as looters and mercenaries in the country of their birth?*

'**REVOLUTION NOW**', is my answer to Tchouteu's question.

The Pride of an African Migrant

PART 3:

THE JOURNEY TO PARADISE

The Pride of an African Migrant

3
FROM CAMEROON TO ENGLAND

Africans in the diaspora often send pictures of themselves riding in very luxurious cars and living in magnificent Western-standard houses. Those who come home for the holidays or for vacation ensure they display wealth from the way they present themselves—always wearing new clothes and looking prim and proper, driving around in newly imported used cars and so on. They make sure that they dominate drinking spots and provide overflowing drinks to those who accompany them to such places. All of these make them the envy of other African families and young men.

On October 25, 2007, I received the go signal for my visa application. The news brought not only an overwhelming joy to the whole family but anticipation and feverish excitement as well. My father pooled all his savings, borrowed money from friends and had us eat plain rice almost every day just to save enough money for my journey. Because we all shared the vision of England as paradise, the entire family sacrificed.

My father's social standing automatically went up in the neighbourhood. He was accorded a lot of respect for having a child go to England and his ability to afford it. The night before I left Cameroon, our family and friends gathered at a farewell party my father had organised.

I finally flew to London two days later. However, I had nowhere to stay and no money to rent a place. All my father's savings were depleted for my visa, leaving nothing much for anything else. Despite all these, however, we stayed steadfast in our dreams of making it big in London, as other people do—or so we thought.

At that time, finding a place to stay was not a priority. The only thing that mattered was to enter England; everything would eventually fall into place. Rent was a luxury we simply could neither afford nor even dare to think about. Nevertheless, my father did manage to provide me with GBP 270 as travel money.

Knowing I had limited money, I thought of how I would cope with my accommodations. There was my friend Bertrand, with whom I attended the same high school back in Cameroon. He had come to London a year before me to pursue his studies. Two days before my departure, I called and briefed him on my trip to London. I told him that I did not have a place to stay. Without any other friend or even acquaintance in Queensland, he was my only hope. Luckily, he agreed to help me out.

On October 28, I arrived at Gatwick Airport, and Bertrand was there to welcome me. As we walked out of the arrival lounge, I told Bertrand that the weather was cold. He smiled and replied that it was still autumn; winter has not even started yet.

He continued to tell me the bad news that he could not give me a place to stay after all because he was already sharing his room with another student. However, Bertrand managed to put me in contact with somebody who could take me in for the night at least. The morning after, I had to attend my first day at the college to register. That very same day, I received a call from a family member's contact who offered me a place to stay for two months.

I visited beautiful places such as the London Eye, Buckingham Palace, Tower Bridge, Oxford Circus and Trafalgar Square as well as fancy restaurants and boutiques and so on. London felt like a fantasy land—an amusement park of sorts. Buildings were towering in the distance, flashy cars passing by and beautiful people in every corner. Indeed, London looked like paradise on Earth. The things I saw reinforced my preconceived assumption that everyone in England is happy, and assured me that I would be satisfied as well. I, however, did not see parts of London like Brixton, Peckham and Hackney—best likened to black ghetto communities. I did not see the harsh realities that were the lives of some African migrants. I was deluded and wholly separated from reality in the same way British people are deluded in their visions of Africa.

Lions, monkeys, jungles and people making fire with stones make up the classic African imagery recognised worldwide. But many Africans have never even seen a lion. Africans supposedly live in caves like the primordial man, and tree branches like monkeys. On top of that, the English media's coverage of Africa and its people are often negative, revolving around issues such as civil war, genocide, famine, poverty and AIDS. While these are indeed major concerns of the continent, they coexist with a plethora of positive news and events that, interestingly, are never reported by Western media.

The intense negative media—being the most consistent contact most Europeans have with Africa—creates assumptions that determine how Africans are perceived in other foreign shores. This explains why many white women claim that all Africans suffer from AIDS because they eat monkeys, which, for them, are the source of AIDS. At that moment, it dawned on me: just like in Africa, education is also a luxury in the United Kingdom.

Another main distinction of the United Kingdom compared to Africa is the freedom exercised by its British political actors. For me, this was suggestive of a civilised government. From the British parliamentary sessions I would often watch on the BBC, I was astonished at how such acts of insubordination can be tolerated—without the deadly consequences as normalised in Africa. When members of the parliament called Gordon Brown, then British Prime Minister, a liar and continued to boo and interrupt him without any hesitation, I was caught in disbelief! In the coming months, having known the indescribable acts of torture committed against asylum seekers in the United Kingdom, I would append a downward review to that first naive impression. The illusion of a civilised government would not only vanish from my mind; it would also awaken me to the reality that British parliament members are just political clowns performing in the circus that is the British parliament and government. It acts as a mere iroko tree shielding an amazon of gross brutality, barbarism and inhumanity.

When the time came for me to leave the place offered to me after two months, I, luckily, managed to get a part-time job in a shop and earned enough to pay my rent. However, it wasn't enough for the tuition fees my college was starting to pester me for. I phoned my father and told him about my predicament. He replied that he did not have any money and that I should be the one sending him money instead to pay back the loans he took for me. Evidently, my father remained deluded. He still believed England to be a place where money falls from trees. I was soon to discover that it was a communally shared social delusion in the African perception of Europe—not a flaw unique to my father.

To pay for my tuition and retain my studentship, I begged my boss to let me work full-time despite it being illegal for someone with a student visa. He took pity on me and allowed me to become a full-time employee. With this new setup, I started missing lectures. Whenever I do make it to class, I was either too tired or distracted. Despite everything, I still could not afford my tuition. So, the next step was clear: save up on rent by requesting to sleep in the shop's restroom, to which my boss agreed.

The shop's restroom was so small that it could not fit even a single bed. The space—or lack thereof—forced me to sleep on the floor with my legs crossed every night. The room did not even have a shower, so during my breaks, I would take a bus to my friend's house, clean myself up and immediately return to work. Despite the hardship, I was thrilled about the support from my boss to the point that I offered to close the shop at 7:00 p.m. on Sundays—five hours more than the usual operating hours. He was delighted.

The Pride of an African Migrant

My boss is Jamaican. He was very proud of his African roots. He always played reggae music in the store, and he was the one who introduced me to the Rastafari movement and reggae music. Before moving to England, my father had actually bought a video CD of Bob Marley and Lucky Dube. I liked watching Marley and Dube jump on the stage; I liked their dreadlocks too. I felt a strong connection with these two artists without understanding whatever they were all singing about as I did not understand English before moving to England. But watching them perform and seeing their emotion on stage, I could definitely sense that what they were all singing about was not just entertainment—it was a serious matter.

I also tried growing my hair in locks like Marley and Dube, but I couldn't as people sporting dreadlocks were not allowed in schools, universities and public offices in my country. Back home, I was denied entry at the University of Buea because my hair was in dreadlocks; a local police station also refused to issue me a national identity card because of my hair. I wrote to the National Commission of Human Rights to complain about the violation of my rights but to no avail.

I did not understand the English language, so I could not understand what Bob Marley and other Jamaican reggae artists were singing about. I was brainwashed to believe that Bob and other Rasta people were just cannabis smokers. My boss always took the time to explain to me each song by Bob Marley. It changed my perception of Rasta people from cannabis smokers to freedom fighters.

Despite my full-time work salary and the free accommodation, I still could not pay my tuition fees.

Eventually, the college decided to expel me following this and my poor attendance. To make matters worse, I was fired after being wrongfully accused of embezzlement, regardless of how much I pleaded.

I firmly believed that I was not sacked because of the money. After all, my boss discovered that a Chinese worker was the one who stole the money and sacked him for that. At that time, I used to believe the real reason I was fired was that my boss has a problem with the African collective memory. He always reminded me that we Africans from the motherland sold them to white people as slaves—he was always bitter about that. This is a widespread Western narrative about transatlantic slave trade to free themselves from the guilt of crime against humanity by the very people who claim to be civilised. Yes, Africans indeed sold other Africans as slaves to whites. However, it is rarely mentioned that for each African sold, five other Africans had to die defending him or her: to sell one African as a slave, they had to kill at least five Africans.

After many years, I now realise that my boss actually did me a great favour by sacking me. If he hadn't, then you would not have been reading this book. The well-known French philosopher Voltaire did after all say in his novel *Candide*: 'All is for the best in the best of all possible worlds'.

Things simply kept on going downhill when my student visa expired. I could not apply for an extension as it would require my college attendance report. What a cycle! I had nothing—no food to eat, no place to stay at and no school to go to. I was left without any other option but to face life on the streets of this paradise that so many people are dying to enter.

In this journey as an irregular immigrant, I met others who were sent to study, their shoulders heavy with the dreams of their families. We numbered in hundreds—dropouts unable to afford education, return home or live with dignity. With the icy English weather, hunger and homelessness, we became animals. It was the survival of the fittest.

PART 4:

PARADISE LOST

The Pride of an African Migrant

4
THE STREET LIFE AND THE COLORISATION OF FEAR

After being sacked from my job, I went to the shop's restroom, picked up my suitcase and headed to the streets. It was so cold. I did not have enough money to afford accommodation. I went to the train station and bought a monthly travel card that cost me almost everything I had. During the day, I would ride on the train to any destination to protect myself from the cold. Later, I would take the same train to return at the very first stop. When the train station closed for the night, I would do the same thing, but this time with a bus. At the last stop, the driver would ask me to leave the bus, and I would wait for the same bus at its first stop.

My suitcase was very heavy and with my new 'lifestyle', it had become a hindrance. I decided to take only what was really necessary: my toothbrush, toothpaste, and perfume. Everything else I threw away—including the suitcase.

After a month, my travel card ran out. I could no longer take refuge in trains or buses, and I had no more money to get by. Unable to get a job and needing money to feed myself, I realised that in this land many considered as paradise, I would have to beg for handouts to fill my stomach. During the day, I begged for money on the streets. I would stay at the library to take refuge from the cold. When the library closed at 7:00 p.m., I would get on a bus using the money I got from begging during the day and went around and around the area. On weekend nights, I would go to a pub to pick up money customers dropped on the floor by the bar counter.

One day, I asked for alms from a black man who reached into his pocket and gave me some money. Suddenly, two men ran up to me, knocked me to the floor and demanded to know what the black man had given to me. I said that he gave me money. They asked what I gave to him in exchange for the money. Out of breath and scared, I explained that I had begged him for money because I was hungry. In not so many words, they said I was lying and accused me of being a drug dealer. They searched me from top to bottom over and over again. When they did not find any drugs on my person, they told me begging is a crime under British law, and then simply walked away.

That was the day I realised the police were watching me—my first encounter with the uniformed illusion of protection.

Another day, I went to visit my friend. He wasn't home, so I waited patiently outside. While waiting, a police car drove up, and officers got out of the vehicle. They walked up to me and said some neighbours called them, telling the police that I was a criminal, so they came to investigate the matter.

Police officers in Europe—and the European society in general—are socially conditioned to perceive black people with suspicion. From the cradle, they are taught that black people are criminals, drug dealers and murderers. This is what led Frantz Fanon, an Afro-Caribbean philosopher, psychiatrist and revolutionary, to note that white and black people are locked in whiteness and blackness, respectively. According to Fanon, the anti-black (racist white) world cannot contain or sustain the affirmation of black life as life, as being or as having a claim on the planet.

In 2011, a 29-year-old black male named Mark Duggan was shot dead by a British policeman on the assumption that he was armed. The incident sparked a nationwide riot, leaving the entire country in a standstill for a week. Shops were destroyed and looted; people were assaulted. Further investigation later revealed that Duggan was, in fact, unarmed. The police opened fire on an unarmed civilian. Was it racially motivated? Most people say 'yes'.

Out of the three officers who killed Mubenga, two had racist messages on their phone, some of which they had distributed widely among their contacts. As New Humanist quoted in its article 'The Death of Jimmy Mubenga: How the UK's Legal System Cast a Black Man beyond Justice':

> Here is one of the 76 texts found on the phone of Terrence Hughes:
>
> 'I went to my local the other day only to find a black barman. So, I said give me a drink nig nog. He said that's a bit racist, come 'round here and see how you like it. So, we swapped places and he said give me a drink you motherfucking white honkey cunt. I said sorry mate; we don't serve niggers!'

The team leader for Mubenga's deportation was Stuart Tribelnig, 39. He had seven racist texts on his phone, all of which he had forwarded to other people...

I walked past a blind black guy begging in the street. He said, 'Any change, mate?' I said, 'Nope, you're still a nigger'.

The judge described the texts as 'grossly offensive and undoubtedly racist'. He, however, did not accept them as evidence in the prosecution of the officers for the death of Mubenga. They were freed and cleared of all charges against them.

Fear and having the wrong perception are the leading causes of discrimination, racism and xenophobia. Simply, they are the manifestation of ignorance.

Fear

We would not call a child 'evil' just because they are afraid to sleep alone in a dark room. Instead, we should first understand that it is natural for the child to be frightened. Second, we should let the child know that there is nothing in the darkness. It's just their mind creating this fear. Third and last, we should switch the light on or come and sleep next to the child to show them that what we are saying is true. Little by little, we'll see that as they grow up, they would be able to get rid of such fear. As a child's unfounded fear of darkness, the US and the UK are also afraid of black people and migrants. There is nothing to be afraid of. This is the same fear that causes police all over the world to kill innocent people and countries to go to war.

Naturally, when fear arises within us, we automatically and unconsciously switch to self-defence mode. Here is when the importance of practising meditation in our daily life comes in. When we sit in meditation, we regularly recognise our thoughts, feelings and emotions as separate from us, creating awareness within us. In our daily life, we are no longer unaware that our thoughts, feelings and emotions are driving us.

Many have said that the killing of Mark Duggan was racially motivated. However, the ideology of racism itself is born out of fear.

Fear not only affects an individual; it also infects an entire nation—even the whole world. We see the government of Israel always in fear of being bombed by Iran. In response to such fear, they want to attack Iran first. They want to convince the whole world that their fear is real as well as their illusions. In his speech at the last UN summit in New York (at the time of writing), Israel's Prime Minister Benjamin Netanyahu, spent all his time talking about his fear and the consequences of Iran acquiring a nuclear weapon. He even presented to the UN assembly a map to show in which stage the Iranian government was in their process of obtaining a nuclear weapon. I called this map a 'map of fear'.

When it comes to fear, we are like children. We should all try our best to handle our fear and understand that the object of our fear is our lack of judgment. Thus, let us have compassion for the victim and the perpetrator, as the venerable Ajahn Sumedho wrote in his book The Four Noble Truths:

'There is fear'. It is just that. The fear that I have experienced is no different from the fear others have. So, this is where we have compassion, even for mangy old dogs. We understand that fear is as horrible for mangy dogs as it is for us.'

Wrong perception

Most of the time, a wrong perception is collective; a result of social conditioning. It is more often how a group of people has been taught by society in which they live to view others and the world around them. White people have wrong perceptions about black people and vice versa. This also applies to other races, even within ethnic groups and gender. Such situation can be likened to what Karl Marx said in A Contribution to the Critique of Political Economy: 'It is not the consciousness of men that determines their being but, on the contrary, their social being that determines their consciousness'.

Through the practice of meditation, we free ourselves from wrong perceptions. From this consciousness as a social being, we attain our true self, which is endowed with infinite compassion.

The venerable Vietnamese Buddhist Master, Thích Nhất Hạnh, organised in his monastery, Plum Village, in France a 'one-week Israel–Palestine retreat'. In this retreat, Israelites and Palestinians learned to live alongside each other. Together, they ate, meditated, and even hugged each other among other things. In the process, both sides recognised what was most important—their fear of each other was merely an illusion. It was, simply, a wrong perception.

5
HOPE AGAIN

I could no longer bear the seemingly endless hardship in the quest for happiness. The English adventure was over; there was nothing left for me in England. With the desire to be simply sent back to my country, I decided to go to the police station and describe my situation.

I reached the station with a long queue of people waiting to be served and sat outside by the doorsteps. There, I met an African street cleaner who looked like he was in his 50s. Perhaps he could see the despair and sorrow on my face when he asked if I was all right. I told him that I was homeless and hungry, and had come to the police station because I wanted to be sent back to my own country. He laughed, asked why I wanted to go back to my country and why I came to England in the first place. I explained everything to him and concluded that, at least, back in my country, I would have a roof over my head. When he asked if I own a property back in Cameroon, I said no. After knowing that I would live in my father's house once I return home, he laughed maniacally. He reminded me that my father's house is not mine. In not so many words, he concluded that even if I returned to Cameroon, I would still be homeless because I did not own any property. When we were done talking, he gave me a GBP 20 note to get myself food and left.

As I watched the man who claimed to be a Nigerian walk away, I came to the decision that I should stay. Like me, he understood that returning home a failure would shame my father, family and friends. Filled with renewed hope and courage, I returned to my life on the streets, begging, sleeping on sidewalks and skipping meals—a true vagabond.

In 2010, I was in Liverpool and ready to return to Cameroon. I had completed the International Organization for Migration's voluntary return application form, and my flight had been booked. Two weeks before my travel date, I had a chance encounter with a mysterious drunk white woman.

It was around 10:00 p.m. I was outside the place I was staying, having just returned from a pub where I had watched the Cameroon football team play at the 19th FIFA World Cup in South Africa. I slipped the key in the lock and was about to open the door when I heard a loud voice call out 'Dready.' I turned around and glanced up and down the street. A few feet away was this white woman, her face flushed and looking tipsy. Her gaze was fixed on me—and I was the only person with dreadlocks within visible distance. I walked the few steps towards the woman and asked how I could help her. It was then I noticed that she had a bottle of whiskey in one hand; she was definitely intoxicated.

'You look like my younger brother', she said.

'Is he black'? I asked.

She replied that he wasn't, but he had long dreadlocks just like mine. I figured she wanted to have a drunken chat, so I told her I wasn't in the mood for a conversation. It was also late, and I needed to rest. Still, she asked if she could accompany me. I was suspicious the whole time.

'What if you call the police claiming rape'? I asked.

She frowned in puzzlement, so I explained: 'That is what white women have been doing to African migrants in this city. I am not judging you, but Liverpool is very racist, and my ancestors say, "The most cowardly birds live the longest".'

She smiled and said that while my ancestors were right, I wasn't a bird but a fearless lion who would live long. When she repeated her request to let her in after assuring me that she had no intent to make any false claims against me to the police, I breathed a sigh of relief. Resigned to whatever fate had designed with this chance encounter, I looked into her dilated eyes and made a final plea: 'I hope I won't end up with a swinging penis for letting you in. My ancestors assert that "The incredulous man returns from the hill of stubborn people with his penis swinging".'

Once inside, I took her bottle of whiskey away and made her a cup of hot tea. I asked for her address and phone number, but she said she had none and was homeless. She asked that I sit next to her while she drank the tea. I obliged. Then, she reached for my hand and asked if I believe in spirituality. I replied affirmatively, and she said she already knew, even stating that I was a spiritual leader.

'You are on a mission in this country, and the mission is not yet over. If you abandon your mission now and return to your country, you will be killed.'

I snatched my palm out of her hand and called her out on her lies, but she looked at me and asked how she could be lying if she knew about my planned return to my country. She proceeded to tell me a secret privy only to me. Still, I remained cynical. Displeased, she stopped the reading as I refused to be honest. I did not own up to the truths, and she left me be. She slept in the house, left early the next day and I never met her again.

Despite my initial cynicism, I was spurred by the encounter and thus paused my planned return to Cameroon. I wanted to discover my mission in the UK. Little did I know that life was about to get more complicated from there on out.

6
TRAPPED BY A GANGSTER

Every day, homeless immigrants and destitute asylum seekers—especially Africans—are dragged into a life of crime. Commercial sex trade, drug trafficking and becoming part of gangs headline what is an infinite spectrum of undesirable activities that these vulnerable groups engage in the quest for survival. I, myself, was picked off the streets and thrust into the world of drug trafficking.

'Please give me GBP 50, so I could call my family back home'.

My gaze darted between the two neatly dressed African men before flitting to the floor—the now-familiar stance of shame and submission. Two low chuckles drew my attention, and my eyes returned up to their faces where their little smirks now grazed on their lips. The pair found something amusing.

To one, I was a junkie. My dreadlocks were a sure sign for him that I wanted the money for marijuana. I ignored their comments, insisting that I genuinely needed the money so I could call home. Eventually, they gave me the needed money, on the condition that they would go with me to the phone booth. I led the way. Some 10 minutes and an international call after, they showed me their genuine smiles. They then told me their names: John and Mark from Tanzania. Upon hearing that they are from Tanzania, I happily shouted 'Julius Nyerere' (Tanzanian anti-colonial activist and politician) and greeted them in Swahili language. The two expressed how glad they were to meet me, and we exchanged phone numbers.

'Hey brother, it's John. Can you take the train to Southend? We got you a place. Someone will pick you up; our brother, Mark'.

It was 9:35 p.m. on that same day, and I had no money to buy a ticket. Still, I ran to the train station. Luckily the gates were wide open; it was great timing. I got on the train despite not purchasing a ticket. Thirty minutes after our train left the station, I asked the passenger beside me how long the trip to Southend would take. I had not been there before; all I knew was that it was one of the Essex County towns. Even with that knowledge, I couldn't recall how I had come about. I probably chalked it up to something I had read somewhere during my daily library warmth-seeking. The man looked at his watch and said we were still half an hour away. My eyes must have popped. I was leaving the streets of London!

At the Southend train station, Mark was waiting for me, a small piece of cardboard in front of his chest with my name scrawled across it. He took me to what he said was John's vacant flat; a place with neither gas nor electricity but a lot warmer than the streets. He lit a candle we found on the table and showed me around, apologising for the state of the flat. I replied that it was a lot better than the streets I was accustomed to. The next morning, there was a knock on the door. It was around 9:00 a.m., and Mark had come to take me to the shop where he got me food, gas and electric card. He loaded the card with some units and informed me that I would need to top them up with my own money subsequently.

A week later, John visited me. He was wearing sunglasses, baggy jeans and heavy chains around his neck. He looked like an American rapper. John then told me that I should quickly search for a job so I could pay him rent. He also told me that he would not be visiting me regularly because he did not live nearby. A week later, John was back. With him were about seven guys, all bearing huge bags of what suspiciously looked like drugs. Every week, they would meet up in the same manner at the flat. One day, John asked if I could sell drugs for him as payment for my rent. Despite the confirmation of John being a drug dealer combined with my fear of having to go back on the streets, I refused.

Another day, John came to me with a business proposal. He asked if I could give him my bank card with my credentials. He told me that he would deposit some money into my account, and we would share the said money. He said it involved no risk but, the more he explained, the more it sounded like fraud to me. I was tempted to refuse again, but I was sure that failure to comply a second time would land me back on London's cold streets. Moreover, he also asked me to find him clients.

A month later, John called very early in the morning to say 4,000 pounds had been deposited into my account. He stated that I was to withdraw it over the counter, and when I expressed my fear of walking into the bank for the transaction, he told me that it was my only option. On my way, John phoned me again and said the ATM confiscated my card because they entered a wrong PIN.

I travelled to London where John and his gang were waiting for me. John then informed me that he has a friend in charge of the payroll of employees of an IT company and that the said friend paid me as if I were working for that company. I asked for the company's name but was not answered. When I mentioned that the bank might ask why I wanted to withdraw such a large amount, they said I should tell them that I wanted to buy a car. My attempts to get more information were rebuffed, so I walked into the bank scared and knees shaking. There was a long queue inside the bank, further intensifying my anxiety. John entered the bank and joined the queue too, lining up right behind me. I got jittery. There was no way I could run.

When it was finally my turn, the cashier peered at me behind her thin, rimmed glasses. I wondered then if she could somehow see my soul.

'What about your card?', she asked.

I told her that the machine had confiscated my card and I didn't know why. She fetched the bank manager who proceeded to probe even deeper about the incident.

He asked me which one of the two ATMs confiscated my card. John did not tell me any details regarding the ATM incident, but I knew I had to be quick and accurate. If I picked the wrong ATM, the bank manager would immediately know something was up. I told the bank manager it was the ATM on his right-hand side. Luckily, I was right. However, the bank manager decided not to return the card until they find out why it was blocked. I told the bank manager I was also there to withdraw money from my account. He asked me to tell him where the money was coming from. I said it was my salary. He wanted to know the name of the company—information that I did not know myself. In the end, the bank manager decided not to give me the money, and so I left the bank empty-handed.

Outside the bank, John and his gang were waiting for me. I explained what happened, and they decided that we should try another bank. When we got there, we were told that the bank had blocked the account for the same reasons. The bank advised that I visit their main branch and speak to the manager. This time, I went to the bank without John or any member of his gang. When I got there, I spoke to the manager. After listening to me, he asked me to wait. After 20 minutes or so, I knew something was wrong, so I decided to leave. However, it was already too late. Just a few minutes down the road, I was intercepted by the police. There was no way I could have run. The police pushed me against the wall and I was immediately handcuffed. They told me that the bank called them and that they had to take me back to the bank for identification. When we arrived at the bank, the bank manager confirmed I was the right suspect, and I was taken to the police station. At the police station, I was told that I was arrested for using someone else's identity. They took my fingerprints as well as a DNA sample. Ten hours later, the police confirmed that it was indeed my identity, and I was finally released.

Despite everything that had happened, John and his gang still wanted me to return to the bank and collect the money. I told them that there was no way on earth I would go back. I was being taken advantage of, simply because I had nowhere to stay, living in a place provided by a drug dealer. I was his prey. Even though I wanted to leave John's place, there was nowhere I could have gone. I was trapped. Although John gave me a place to stay, I still could not find a job. I was still begging on the streets. It was while I was out begging that I came across a man named Millis from Ghana.

I begged him for 50 pence; he gave me a pound. Millis told me that he is a pastor. He invited me to church, and I obliged. After church, Millis would take me to his place and give me something to eat. I explained to him that a drug dealer was taking advantage of the fact that I did not have a place to stay. Although he sympathised, Millis could not do anything because he was also just renting a room. He told me that as long as I went to church, I would be fine. Early in the morning before Millis went to work, he would call me to come and eat at his house. Sometimes, he would even give me food to take home. It was through Millis that I got introduced to a kind person named Abdhi.

Abdhi is a Somalian refugee, and he was renting a flat. He was another person I could rely on. While walking on the street with Abdhi one day, we saw an advertisement on an office window: 'Looking for French-speaking people to work in a call centre; immediate start.' Because I speak French, Abdhi and I walked in, and I applied for the job. Two days later, I was called for an interview, and I got the job. For me, it served as an excellent opportunity to leave John's place. With the job, I could afford my own rent. I phoned John and told him I was leaving his flat. He was so angry that he asked me about his rent money. I told him that he would get it as soon as I was paid.

Now that I finally left his flat, John considered me as his enemy, to the point that he even asked my friend Abdhi to tell me that death was at my door. Two weeks later, at around 9:00 p.m., I heard a loud knock at the door. It was John and his gang; they managed to find me. As soon I opened the door, John jumped on me, pushed me against the wall and swore to kill me if I did not pay him rent. I was lucky that my housemate called the police. When John and his gang heard the police siren, they fled.

While John had taken me away from the cold streets of London, he did not really help me. He was merely an opportunist, using helpless illegal and irregular immigrants on their quest for happiness and as they try to make ends meet in England. All those working for John were undocumented immigrants and destitute asylum seekers. Later, I heard that the police arrested and jailed some of John's gang members who were undocumented immigrants and destitute asylum seekers for drug trafficking. They would eventually be deported back to their countries.

A few years from that time, I recall a period when I was also homeless. Another drug dealer offered me accommodation in exchange for drug handling. He said his place was only used for drug storage, housing huge amounts of cannabis, heroin and cocaine from time to time. I gambled and took the risk of living in such a place just because I was a homeless, irregular immigrant. My presence alone at that storehouse could have led me to jail even though I was not at all involved in the trade. No police officer would have believed that the drugs were not mine, that I had nothing to do with everything that was happening and that I was only there because I had nowhere else to go. How do we expect destitute asylum seekers in the UK to survive when drug trafficking is the only option being offered to them?

'Drug mules are not criminals. They are just unemployed people. When I was just eight years old, my father was sentenced in the USA for drug trafficking, but he was not a criminal.'

—Rafael Correa, Ecuadorian president

7
A SHADOW OF HAPPINESS

My family was not happy at all with my wretched situation. They considered me a failure because I could not send them money. A person living in England and not succeeding in life was far beyond their imagination. For them, anyone living in England should have the means to make it.

However, everything changed when I managed to land the call centre job. After calling my family in Cameroon to tell them about my new job—my own desk, a suit to go to work, and being able to send them money for the first time—they were all incredibly happy. I got to promise them that I would be sending them money every month. But it was not actually just my family. I was also overjoyed. At that time, however, I did not know that what I thought was happiness was only excitement—a shadow of joy.

It did not last long. After a couple of months working at the call centre, they discovered that I did not have the proper documents to work. I was fired. Without a job, I could no longer afford my rent. I had to face life on the streets once again—something I thought that I would never have to experience ever again.

The Pride of an African Migrant

PART 5:

HUMAN RIGHTS

The Pride of an African Migrant

8
SEEKING ASYLUM

Once more, I was homeless. There were instances in which my friend Abdhi would allow me to sleep at his flat, but they were far and few. There was a small storeroom for a boiler just outside Abdhi's flat. It was quite tiny; even one person could barely fit inside. Unknown to Adhi, I would sneak into the small storeroom at night and sleep there. The temperature was so low in that room that I had to wear two pairs of jeans and three jackets every time I would sleep there. My life seemed just to keep getting more and more difficult—I felt trapped.

With those thoughts in mind, I decided to seek asylum in England. I thought it would be best to get help from the government and live a happy life. All my life, I had never been involved in politics. Moreover, I had no fear of returning to Cameroon. As many of us do, I believed in the illusion that joy, happiness and a better future could only be found in a developed country such as England. I was ready to go to extremes to find that elusive happiness even if I had to sabotage my own country.

Refusing to sleep one more night on the streets, I headed to the Home Office in London to seek asylum. When I got there, I found that they had airport-style surveillance. Moreover, there were at least 250 people—children and men and women of all ages—queuing up to seek asylum. I was told that it was like this every day. Most could barely speak English. They were from different races and nationalities. Their faces only showed despair, sorrow and anger. For them, the UK was the only place where they could have all the things they couldn't have in their own countries. It was the place to live a happy life. After living in the UK for three years at that time, I realised that the only things I could get there were homelessness, hunger and the need to beg on the street. For some reason though, I still had a bit of hope.

After waiting for more than three hours, it was my turn to be registered as an asylum seeker. Then, we were taken to a Catholic church where we spent the night. At the church, I shared a room with an asylum seeker from Rwanda. He told me he had been living in England for 10 years, and that for more than 3 years back then he had been locked up in detention centres. I asked him what a detention centre is and why they had to lock him up there for more than three years. He told me that a detention centre is a prison for asylum seekers and irregular immigrants who refuse to return voluntarily to their countries. At first, I did not believe his story. After all, England has been portrayed as a country where human rights and democracy are held in the highest regard.

The next morning, we were given temporary accommodation in Liverpool. At least 200 people were living there, however, as we had to share rooms with other asylum seekers. Later, we had a meeting with the head of the staff. He explained that it was part of our human rights to seek asylum in the UK; however, 9 out of 10 cases still get rejected. After my two-week stay at the temporary housing, I was given a more permanent place to stay, which was also in Liverpool. I was to stay there for three months while my asylum case was being processed.

At the new place, I shared rooms with Cedric from Zimbabwe, Jonas from Eritrea and Lee from China—all of whom were extremely nice people. Out of the three, Cedric and I got along very well because he was the only one who spoke English.

I arrived at the permanent accommodation on a Saturday, the same day I had a conversation with Cedric. He told me about the difficulty of seeking asylum in the UK: he stayed in England for nine years and has been staying in detention centres for more than a year. Despite all this, he still had not been granted a stay in the UK. I told Cedric that it was the second time I had heard this kind of story. I did not believe it because, for me, the UK was a model of human rights. Cedric laughed and said that come Monday, he would take me to a place called Asylum Link. There, I could meet other asylum seekers and listen to their stories. Upon hearing that, I could not wait for the weekend to end. I wanted to listen to these people's stories.

The only thing I knew about the city of Liverpool was Liverpool Football Club. In fact, our accommodation was located in Anfield—the home of the aforementioned football club. I asked Cedric about life in Liverpool and what to expect. 'Expect racism. Black people are not welcome here', Cedric replied. A week later, while walking on the street, eggs were thrown at me—a reminder that I was, indeed, not welcome.

I found racism in Liverpool very strange because the city had an encounter with black people for many centuries. Liverpool was known as the leading British slave-trading port. In particular, more than 1.5 million enslaved Africans passed through the city's ports.

Given this history, the city tries to fight racism by exposing its people to African history and culture through various initiatives, such as Liverpool's International Slavery Museum and the annual week-long Africa Oyé Festival, the largest celebration of live African music in the United Kingdom.

The Saturday I arrived, Cedric and I visited the National Museum in Liverpool, where I saw the mummy of a Pharaoh for the first time. I was delighted when the museum guide told me that the mummy is that of a black Pharaoh. This is rarely acknowledged as the ideology of racism ignores or marginalises the contributions, achievements and history of black people. 'The tragedy of Africa is that the African has not fully entered into history,' said former French President Nicolas Sarkozy in an address at Dakar's main university. Meanwhile, British historian Trevor Roper said, 'Africa has no history'.

Early on Monday, I knocked on Cedric's door and we headed to Asylum Link. It was a 40-minute walk from our accommodation. Asylum Link is a St. Anne's Church charity devoted to helping asylum seekers. It was the only place in Liverpool where destitute asylum seekers could eat, clothe themselves, play table tennis, learn how to cook English food, play music and use the computer, among other things—for free. Asylum Link also provides free English classes for asylum seekers who were unable to speak the language. In fact, Asylum Link was the day centre for homeless asylum seekers.

Upon arriving, we were greeted by a barrage of asylum seekers. Everyone seemed to speak a different language, with people grouped into either by nationality or a common language. What they all had in common, however, was the despair and sorrow on their faces. They were all praying for one thing: for the British government to grant them asylum in the UK. For them, the UK is the best place to be. Cedric quickly showed me around the place, where to get food to eat and clothes to wear as well as the registrar's office. Now was the perfect time for me to listen to stories of other asylum seekers.

I was first introduced to a Cameroonian asylum seeker named Dominick. He had been living in the UK for eight years and still had not been granted asylum. To know more about detention centres, I asked Dominick if what I had heard recently about such centres in the UK were true.

Dominick told me about his first arrest by the UK Home Office where he was put in a detention centre for six months. After his stay in the detention centre, they wanted to deport him back to Cameroon. When he refused, the British immigration officers savagely beat, tortured and forcibly placed him on a plane to Cameroon via France. Upon his arrival in France, the French officials cancelled Dominick's flight to Cameroon and sent him back to the UK because he did not have a Cameroonian passport. To have Dominick deported, the UK Home Office issued him a European travel document even though he was not European. Although he was later released, he found himself destitute again with no place to stay and no food to eat. He had to struggle on his own.

The second time Dominick was arrested by the UK Home Office, he was placed back in another detention centre. His second arrest landed him another six-month stint because he refused his deportation again. Once again, Dominick was savagely beaten and tortured. This time, the beatings left him with a fracture on his right arm. When he was released, the same cycle happened again: a destitute without food to eat nor place to stay. He had to struggle on his own again. Dominick's story left me in shock.

Two weeks later, Dominick introduced me to another asylum seeker from Cameroon. Her name is Beatrice.

Beatrice told me that despite her extended stay in the UK, she still had not been granted asylum. She also described her fear of going back to her home country. According to Beatrice, the UK Home Office arrested her and placed her in a detention centre where she stayed for months and months. Similar to Dominick, Beatrice also refused her deportation. Her refusal earned her a savage and merciless beating from the British immigration officers. The encounter left her disfigured, and while she was still unconscious, was sent back to Cameroon.

When Beatrice arrived at the Douala International Airport in Cameroon, she was still unconscious after the more than eight-hour flight. Just imagine how savagely she was beaten. At the airport in Douala, they denied Beatrice's entry for two reasons: she was still unconscious, and Cameroonian officers discovered that the British immigration officers faked a Cameroonian passport to have her deported. Moreover, the

British immigration officers attempted to bribe the Cameroonian airport authorities, telling them that Beatrice sabotaged the president of Cameroon to the British authorities as well, even revealing her asylum case and thus putting her life at higher risk.

As a rule of International law, asylum seekers enjoy a right of confidentiality. The information in an application for asylum, including the fact that an individual applied for asylum, shall be kept confidential.

By revealing Beatrice's asylum application, the British immigration officers breached the confidentiality of asylum applications. To their dismay, all their efforts still failed. Beatrice was taken back to the UK. She was destitute: nowhere to stay and no food to eat. When Beatrice finished telling me her story, I found myself in tears. I actually had to say to her that I had heard enough and did not want to hear more.

On TV, powerful countries like England say that corruption, political instability and civil wars are some of the reasons why poverty exists in Africa—which is true. They also say that they are trying their best to eradicate corruption in Africa. But how can this statement be true when the UK Home Office bribes African officers every single day, creating fraudulent documents such as fake passports. A British immigration officer revealed to me that when they have to deport immigrants without travel documents, most of the time, they bring presents to their local authorities to facilitate their entry back to the countries they believe that they are from.

Asylum seekers are not only unlawfully deported in the UK; they are also deported to countries they do not belong to.

Such a situation has been made possible by a bribing system. For instance, given that one out of four Africans is Nigerian, the UK Home Office immediately concludes that someone speaking Pidgin English is Nigerian. With this assumption, Cameroonians, Ghanaians and others who speak Pidgin English with no document to prove their nationality are simply deported to Nigeria. However, Pidgin English is not only spoken in Nigeria. All Anglophone countries in West Africa speak the language: Cameroon, Nigeria, Ghana, Liberia and Sierra Leone.

This bribing system has been in operation for some time now. Similar events have occurred, even way back in the 60s with the French government making fake Conakry Guinea banknotes just to destabilise Conakry's prosperous economy— as if slavery and colonisation were not enough. After destabilising our economy, they come and lend us money with high interest rates. When unable to pay back, they take our mineral resources and control our government policies.

It is in this sense that Ken Jones wrote in The New Social Face of Buddhism that the 'International Monetary Fund could be considered as a terrorist organization'. Furthermore, 'The International Monetary Fund... regularly coerces poor debtor countries with threats of withholding further aids unless they adopt draconian domestic policies concerning social programs and welfare services. These have been shown to have predictably violent impacts upon the poor, including increased child mortality and reduced life expectancy'.

I met with other asylum seekers who stayed in detention centres. They told me that sleeping tablets and certain drugs were sneaked into the meals of asylum seekers who refuse to return voluntarily to their countries. Some would then be deported unconscious to their countries. Other asylum seekers in detention centres thus refused to eat, fearing that they might be drugged and be deported unconsciously. According to a detention officer I talked to, 'those who refuse to eat are taken to a location where they would be force-fed.'

I also met asylum seekers with electronic tags chained around their legs like dogs, allowing the UK Home Office to monitor them 24/7. They did not deserve that. Asylum seekers are not criminals.

During my stay at Campsfield House, an immigration detention centre in Oxfordshire, many asylum seekers were tagged with a condition for their temporary release. It was but a trap and a way to send them to prison later on. Temporarily released with a tag around their legs but with no place to stay, support and authorisation to work, they were left without a choice but to survive on the street stealing from shops and selling drugs. Once caught, they would find themselves sent back to prison. It was all but an illusion—pseudo liberty.

Aside from adults, little children are also kept in detention centres in the UK as well just because their parents are irregular immigrants or failed asylum seekers. These children have no right to education or even to play—they are locked up within the centres' four walls.

Every day, we would see BBC adverts that state 'EVERY SINGLE CHILD HAS THE RIGHT TO PLAY'. It's not something we see on the BBC alone. Similar messages can be seen in supermarkets, on the streets, almost everywhere in the UK. I would love to know to whom the British government is addressing this message. Is it to poor little children in Africa or to those locked up in detention centres in the UK? Bob Marley's '*Slogans*' echo these sentiments:

> *Can't take your slogans no more*
> *Wipe out the paintings of slogans all over the streets,*
> *confusing the people while your asphalt burns our tired feet*
> *I see borders and barriers,*
> *segregation, demonstrations and riots...*
> *A-sufferation [suffering] of the refugees*

This was sung 40 years ago, and yet nothing has really changed. They keep on writing the same slogans, the same lies. These stories had a big effect on how I felt about England at that time. I was very shocked that something like this could happen in a country like England, a country that was so outspoken about human rights.

After this, I decided not to listen to the news again. In particular, I avoided the BBC. It seemed to me that the BBC would only report when British soldiers are killed in a conflict zone, when British tourists are kidnapped. They fail to report when asylum seekers are savagely and mercilessly brutalised and even killed in the UK by the UK border regime. The BBC lets the world know what happens in other countries, but they never let the world know what happens in the UK. They do not even inform the British citizens of what happens in their own country.

The television is just another weapon of mass destruction. The only thing they can do is distort the truth and create hatred. They are not vehicles for appreciative inquiry. It is in this vein that I believe we should depend on alternative sources for our news. Media programs the way we think. They tell us who the perpetrators are and who the victims are. Each time we listen, we have to filter information. The news we receive on TV depends on who broadcasts it and influences how we perceive other people. As Canadian philosopher Marshall McLuhan has said, 'The medium is the message'.

Psychologists conducted an experiment to show how the media can even influence what we see. The experiment was about people who witnessed a fight. One of the men engaged in the fight wore a red cap. The media reported on TV that he wore a black cap. Then, the witnesses were asked if what was reported on TV regarding the colour of the cap was true. Most of them said yes.

The Pride of an African Migrant

9
INTERNATIONAL REFUGEE WEEK

For the 2012 International Refugee Week, I was invited to Liverpool John Moores University to raise awareness about asylum seekers, as well as raise funds for destitute asylum seekers. I noticed that almost all students in the hall that day had wrong perceptions and a prejudiced view of asylum seekers. For them, asylum seekers were simply economic migrants who came to the UK to snatch jobs from them.

These students were victims of mass media and politicians who all claim that asylum seekers are economic migrants. Politicians in Europe and America use immigration issues to win elections—the perfect breeding ground for xenophobia. Politicians claim that they have to get their countries rid of immigrants to eradicate unemployment, insecurity and much more. They make their citizens perceive asylum seekers and immigrants as a threat to their well-being.

At the hall, most students did not even know what an asylum seeker is or how people become asylum seekers. They were unaware of the difference between an 'asylum seeker' and a 'refugee'. The only thing they knew about asylum seekers was that they are economic migrants who came to take their jobs away.

For African migrants, to trek the world's largest desert, swim the dreadful Mediterranean Sea, and come to Europe and take European jobs just means that Europeans are indolent—the main reason they needed slaves to build their cities and create their wealth.

The topic of my speech then was 'Mind Fuckers'. Here is an excerpt of the said speech I delivered before the students of Liverpool John Moores University for the 2012 International Refugee Week.

> *I will start by apologizing because there will be swear words in my speech. However, I don't have a choice. There is no other way I can put it. Today, I will be talking about 'mind fuckers'. Who are they? They are mass media, religious leaders and politicians who want us to believe what they want us to believe and who want us to think about what they want us to think. They have put our minds in captivity. Politicians have all agreed to put confusion and fear in our minds by means of [the] media. Politicians want you to believe that asylum seekers are here to take your jobs away. What you know about asylum seekers is what your government wants you to know. Asylum seekers are people who have left their countries to save their own lives, and in this country, asylum seekers are neglected.*
>
> *Most asylum seekers are destitute. They have no accommodation, they have no food to eat, they are chased by the UK border agency and they do not even have the right to learn English as soon as they are*

destitute. They pick up the English language on the streets. Asylum seekers have no other choice than to get involved in prostitution, drugs, and shoplifting. In my experience, I have also been forced to steal my way out of hunger. Asylum seekers go after refuge in your country because your country sells guns to their governments and also to rebels. We do not manufacture guns in Africa. However, Africa is full of guns. Your government supports dictatorial regimes to provide you with mineral resources and raw materials and is not willing to support asylum seekers. Keep calm, more asylum seekers are coming. I want you to be aware of mind fuckers. I want you to filter what you hear from the BBC...

The Pride of an African Migrant

10
JIMMY MUBENGA: A MARTYR OF GLOBALISATION

> I and I plant the corn
> Didn't my people before me
> Slave for this country
> Now you look at me with a scorn
> Then you eat up all my corn
> Build your penitentiary, we build your schools
> Brainwash education to make us the fools
> Hate is your reward for our love
> —Bob Marley

One morning, when I arrived at Asylum Link, nobody was playing table tennis. It was silent. Nobody was talking. The silence was absolute and unusual. Not trying to break the silence, I asked asylum seekers what was going on, and they showed me a newspaper. From the newspaper, I found out that a 46-year-old Angolan asylum seeker named Jimmy Mubenga, who spent two years in a detention centre, was killed on 12 October 2010 whilst resisting deportation from the UK. All this happened while his flight to Luanda was preparing for take-off from the Heathrow airport in London. Mubenga lived in the UK for at least 16 years and was forced to leave behind a wife and five children.

Back in 2010, then British Prime Minister David Cameron pledged to reduce migration into Britain during his campaign—'no ifs, no buts'—and announced a series of radical new measures. I followed his campaigns and debates on TV. Now, these are the questions I would like Mr Cameron to answer:

What did he mean by reducing migration into Britain, 'no ifs, no buts'?

Did he mean to kill migrants, torture them or just have them deported?

Scientists, through technology and the internet, have largely contributed to make this world a global village. However, politicians like Mr Cameron, do not seem to have the same objective. The globalisation that they talk about is just another lie they are selling to developing countries—another form of colonisation.

Mubenga was tortured and killed just because he wanted to stay in a country that his forefathers built and lost their lives for in their efforts to save England from the German atrocity during the First and Second World War. African soldiers were forced to fight for their colonial masters. The British fought alongside African troops against the Germans.

Nick Dearden, director of the UK campaigning organisation, Global Justice Now, reminds us that, 'The City of London (where Mubenga was tortured and killed) is awash with profits extracted from the land and labour of Africa'. In her article, we find Dr Priyamvada Gopal sharing the same view: 'Much of Britain's wealth is built on slavery. So why shouldn't it pay reparations?'

> 'The Industrial Revolution would have been impossible without the wealth generated by slave labour. Britain's major ports, cities and canals were built on invested slave money. Several banks can trace their origins to the financing of the slave trade. Apart from the Barclays Brothers, who were slave traders, we also know of Baring and HSBC, which can be traced back to Thomas Leyland's banking house. The Bank of England also had close connections to the trade. Hundreds of Britain's great houses were built with the wealth of slavery, and the Church of England also acknowledges its pecuniary gains from slavery. As an excellent project at University College London is showing, not only many contemporary millionaires and politicians but also perfectly ordinary middle-class people come from families, which were compensated for the loss of slaves. The freed slaves, of course, never received such compensation and their families inherited; instead, the poverty and landlessness [which] blights them to this day. Capitalism itself, along with cheap beach holidays, would have been impossible without slavery.'

However, this has already been forgotten. Bob Marley makes us remember in his song *'Crazy Baldheads'*.

> *I and I plant the corn*
> *Didn't my people before me*
> *Slave for this country*
> *Now you look at me with a scorn*

Then you eat up all my corn
Build your penitentiary
We build your schools
Brainwash education
To make us the fools
Hate is your reward for our love

I was very shocked. I tried to gather asylum seekers to protest outside the Home Office in Liverpool but to no avail. They all let their fear get the best of them. It was then that I decided to protest on my own outside the Home Office in Liverpool. I wanted to leave the UK with pride and dignity, and to show my pride for all asylum seekers. I picked up a placard at Asylum Link on which I wrote the following message: 'STOP KILLING ASYLUM SEEKERS. WE NEED JUSTICE FOR JIMMY MUBENGA'.

I went with that placard on my own to the Home Office in Liverpool. When I reached the area, I stood outside and started protesting on my own. Later, the head of immigration personnel came out and asked me to stop. I simply ignored him. People who were passing by stopped and listened to me. They were all taken aback by what had happened in their country and the fact that they have not heard about any of what I was sharing on any TV show.

After four hours of solitary demonstration, I left and went home. The next day, I continued my peaceful protest still outside the Home Office in Liverpool. This time, however, the police were called after just half an hour of protesting. When the police arrived, they asked me what I was doing. I told them I was protesting against the killing of asylum seekers by the British government. The police told me to stop, but I replied by asking them if I was not entitled to freedom of speech. They did not answer me. They simply knocked me to the floor, handcuffed me and took me to the station.

I could not believe that any person could lose freedom of speech in a country like England, a country that talks so much about the right of speech. Upon our arrival at the police station, I was charged for public disorder. I asked the policemen who arrested me if they saw me causing any public nuisance. Again, there was no response. I believed the problem lies not it me being a public nuisance but related to preserving the illusion of a fair system.

All my clothes were removed, and I was thrown into a freezing cell bare naked. An hour later, a psychiatrist came to see me. He told me that he was there to take me to the hospital as the police had told him that I was mentally disturbed. I told the psychiatrist that I was not and that I was arrested while peacefully protesting outside the Home Office for the killing of an asylum seeker. I told him it was all a trick the police used to shut me up. After I finished my story, the psychiatrist concluded that he could not take me to the hospital because I was not mentally disturbed. When he left, I was taken back to my freezing cell.

The British police called a psychiatrist because, in their minds, a person must be deranged, deluded and in need of psychiatric assistance if they are protesting for human rights—even though we hear the British government talk about human rights every single day on TV. However, why does the British government support the 'mentally disturbed' Libyans and Syrians in seeking human rights and democracy? Do they not need to be given psychiatric care by the British government instead of weapons to overthrow their governments and kill each other?

The next morning, I was taken to court for my hearing. I had a meeting with a solicitor who suggested that I plead guilty for public nuisance so that I could get away with a noncustodial sentence. I told the solicitor there was no way on earth that I would plead guilty to something I did not do. After that meeting, I was taken before the judge. I pleaded not guilty for public nuisance, and the judge adjourned the court. The judge told me not to protest again outside the Home Office, or I would be arrested again. I was also instructed to report twice a week at the local police station. I asked the judge why I could not peacefully protest outside the Home Office and about my right to do so because of freedom of speech. The judge replied: 'It's not about freedom of speech. It's just how things are'. Again, I cannot understand the British law. I was told not to protest again outside the Home Office, a public place. If I do so, I would be arrested again.

Despite their instructions, I decided to continue my protest right after I left the court. This time, I printed the same note that was on my placard, and glued it on the back of my jacket. I wore the jacket every day so that people could see. During the day, I would go and stand for hours in the town centre wearing my jacket. After some time, I started getting threats because of what I was wearing—specifically, of what was on my jacket.

At around 10:00 p.m., the accommodation I was staying was set on fire. Clearly, it was a plot to kill me. I managed to escape with the other asylum seekers with whom I was sharing the place with. The fire brigade was called, and they responded quickly and aggressively. The firefighters confirmed that it was an attempted murder, and they called the police to come and investigate. When the police arrived, I was taken to the police station, where I was told to get rid of the note on the back of my jacket. From that moment, I understood why they tried to kill me. I was now getting scared. Moreover, I was in this fight on my own. In an effort to gain support, I wrote so many times to human rights organisations. However, none of them got back to me. Later, I was invited to a radio show to speak about problems faced by asylum seekers, but I was so scared to attend the show that I decided not to go through with it. With my life at risk, I decided to flee from Liverpool.

At least four weeks later in London, there was a big demonstration against the killing of Mubenga. At the same time, students were also protesting in London against the rise of university fees. No television had covered the demonstration regarding the killing of Mubenga. They all preferred to cover the students' protest. This just means that the killing of an asylum seeker, of a black man, of an African, and of an Angolan is insignificant compared to the increase in university fees.

Human rights and democracy are endless endeavours that allow no one to claim to be the pinnacle or the model.

The Pride of an African Migrant

11
FLEEING FROM LIVERPOOL

After the murder attempt on me failed, I decided to flee from Liverpool and return to Southend. Before leaving the city of Liverpool, I managed to get a Belgian passport from a friend of a friend. Originally, the passport belonged to a Congolese naturalised Belgian. The photo on the passport was just like my own—it was impossible to see the difference.

In Southend, none of my friends would offer me accommodation. I had to face the street life again, but at that point, it had become second nature for me. I no longer felt ashamed for begging on the streets. I continued sleeping in the tiny boiler room outside my friend's house without his knowledge. During the day, I would beg for some money to eat and then spend my day at the library. On Sundays, I attended church. Food would be offered after every service, and I would eat. That was why I would attend at least three different churches every Sunday—to take advantage of the food provided.

While begging on the streets, I came across a Kenyan named Samuel. I told Samuel about my experience in Liverpool, how I was fed up living in England, and how I plan to return to my own country. Samuel let out a chuckle and told me that he had been living in England for the last 12 years and yet he still has not been granted asylum in the UK. He also told me he was kept in detention centres for more than two years. Later, he said that he was transferred to HM Prison Brixton in London with other asylum seekers because they protested against the death of a Senegalese asylum seeker who committed suicide in a detention centre. After that conversation, Samuel took me to a pub and offered me a drink. At the pub, he told me to be strong and not give up. For him, England is still the best place to be. Before parting with Samuel that day, he told me I could go to his house any weekend to get food.

My friend Samuel and the other asylum seekers who protested because of the Senegalese asylum seeker's suicide in the detention centre officially became prisoners in the prison even though they were already prisoners in detention centres. The British system did not consider them as prisoners because, in the eyes of their government, detention centres are not prisons. They are removal centres. However, if detention centres are not considered as prisons in the UK, why should asylum seekers and irregular immigrants be kept in detention for years and years? Moreover, asylum seekers and irregular immigrants in the UK can be held in such centres for an indeterminate period, to the point that some would be held there for more than six years.

This is in no way mere detention. It is imprisonment.

Around that time, the UK Home Office arrested Dominick again—the third time—and was put back in detention. He was lucky this time because he was neither beaten nor brutalised.

Because he had a child with a regular immigrant in the UK, he was just held in detention and released after only six weeks. His release came after the judge deemed it unfair to separate the child from his father. This was a rare case. Many asylum seekers have actually been deported regardless of having children in the UK.

Several provisions within the 1989 Convention on the Rights of the Child, ratified by the UK, address the rights of children to be with their parents and grow up in a family environment:

- Article 7 guarantees the right to know and be cared for by his or her parents.
- Article 8 guarantees the right to family relations without interference.
- Article 9 bans separation of parents from children, except when competent authorities subject to judicial review determine, in accordance with applicable laws and procedures, that such separation is necessary for the best interests of the child.

Dominick called me from the detention centre. He told me that he was sharing his room with a Jamaican, who has been held in detention for more than six years already. According to Dominick, the Jamaican was neither an irregular immigrant nor a failed asylum seeker: he was being held for no valid reason. It was said that he committed a crime in the UK, but I did not get to know the exact details. He was found guilty of the crime and was sentenced to prison. At this point, it should be mentioned that in the UK, getting on a bus or a train without a ticket can be considered a crime. After he did his time in prison, he was transferred to detention centre after detention centre. The British government attempted to have him deported back to Jamaica, but for diplomatic reasons, it did not work. This is how the Jamaican has been held illegally in detention centres in a country that speaks greatly about human rights.

The case of the Jamaican confirms findings of a commissioned review of the UK government: 'there are still many people in detention who should not be there'.

The powerful British government fears the release of the Jamaican because of the possibility that he may commit a new crime. He is considered a danger to society. When British-born or white British citizens commit crimes in the UK, they are simply released after serving their time, carrying on with their usual lives. Why can it not be the same for the Jamaican?

While staying at Campsfield House, I met a French-born Congolese who was also held illegally in detention centres. Like the Jamaican, he also committed a crime and was sentenced for it. He did his time in prison and was subsequently transferred to a detention centre. However, when he asked to be deported back to his country, France, the British authority denied his request. The reason was the possibility that he would come back to the UK to see his family. But, is it a crime to see one's own family? Is it not a basic principle of human rights?

I would love the British government to know that in life, nothing is static, unchangeable, or permanent. We all learn from our mistakes. Our past does not define who we will be tomorrow. Everything changes, moment after moment. I know for a fact that the British government is changing too, and I wish that one day, it will truly become what it speaks and claims to be on TV—a government wherein human rights prevail.

Following the truth that everything changes at every moment, a criminal record cannot be applied to reality. All over the world, criminals and offenders are given criminal records that hinder them from getting jobs in the future, in the process denying them a chance to change their lives. A man who committed a crime yesterday is not the same man today. At each moment, our body changes. Cells in our body die and get reborn every second—we can absolutely say that we are not the same person we were a minute ago. This is the same with our minds. Our mind also changes at each moment, following the circumstances we are faced with.

Systems all over the world deny criminals and offenders new opportunities, thinking that they are still the same people, the same culprits society has labelled them as. However, by doing this, criminals and offenders will only remain as they are—as what systems want them to be.

> 'The goal of society is to provide favourable conditions for each person... and this must be the most important function of government.'
>
> —Nagarjuna, Indian Buddhist sage

> 'The degree of civilization in a society can be judged by entering its prisons.'
>
> —Fyodor Dostoevsky

The Pride of an African Migrant

PART 6:

SOUL'S JOURNEY

The Pride of an African Migrant

12
SARAH JANE

I was an irregular immigrant. I had no place to stay. From time to time, friends offered me their place. However, because of my situation, I decided to go to nightclubs in an effort to look for British women who would find me interesting and give me a place to stay. It was my only chance to escape the street life in the UK. As an irregular immigrant in the UK, it was the only way to survive. British women were the only option, and they were our preys.

Most of my friends were involved with British women. We did not care about their physical appearance—age, body, or looks. Most importantly, we did not care about love. What was most important was to have a British woman who would put you up and get you off the street. It was part of our plan to get them pregnant as soon as possible, which would give us a chance to remain in the country legally.

This is the life of most African migrants—one without pride and dignity.

Every weekend, I would go to nightclubs. On one of those nights, a beautiful blonde woman took notice of me and approached me. As she stood right in front of me, I noticed a Bob Marley tattoo on her right harm. Her name is Sarah Jane, and she was 38 then.

Straight away, I asked if she likes reggae music. 'Yes, I do, and I am a Rasta', she replied. Then, she started singing 'Slavery Days', a song by reggae legend Burning Spear.

> *Do you remember the days of slavery?*
> *Do you remember the days of slavery?*
>
> *And how they beat us*
> *And how they worked us so hard*
> *And they used us*
> *'Till they refuse us*
>
> *Do you remember the days of slavery?*
>
> *And a big fat bull*
> *We usually pull it everywhere*
> *We must pull it*
> *With shackles around our necks*
> *And I can see it all no more*
>
> *Do you remember the days of slavery?*
>
> *My brother feels it*
> *Including my sisters too*
> *Some of us survive*
> *Showing them that we are still alive*
>
> *Do you remember the days of slavery?*

History can recall, history can recall
History can recall the days of slavery
Oh, slavery days! Oh, slavery days!

While I remember, please remember
Try to remember my brother, my sister

Hearing this white woman sing *'Slavery Days'* left me in awe. I could not believe that a white woman, even if she claims to be a Rastafari, would dare sing this song before a black man, especially one with dreadlocks. I wasn't fully convinced that she was a real Caucasian woman. I thought she was simply an alienated black woman with low self-esteem who bleached her skin and wore a wig on her head—like black women who hate themselves do. If she were the white woman as she appears to be, she could not be racist.

I asked her, 'Are you not worried that you might be labelled as a racist just by singing 'Slavery Days'? She replied, 'How is it racist to recall one's own history? Slavery is not only the history of black people but also that of white people'.

Although slavery is part of our common history—later having talked with one of her daughters, I realised that she knows nothing about slavery—when I asked her why, I found out that slavery is not discussed in school.

That night, I did not immediately reveal my real identity to Sarah. I introduced myself as a Belgian; I speak English with a French accent as French is my second language compared to English which is my third language. It was only much later on that I would reveal my real identity and situation in the UK to Sarah.

The Pride of an African Migrant

That night, Sarah and I talked as if we were old friends. Sarah was falling in love, little by little. But I was not interested in love. What I needed was a woman who could offer me a place to stay. Later that night, Sarah told me that she has two daughters, aged 11 and 13. She also mentioned that she and her husband were separated. I would later find out that she lied. Sarah had to go to work the next morning but told me that she would meet up with me on her days off, Tuesdays and Fridays. We exchanged mobile numbers, and I sent her off in a taxi. The very same night, Sarah paged me when she arrived home.

After that, Sarah and I began paging each other every day. A week after, Sarah and I met again. She took me to a pub. There, she confessed that she was still living with her husband, but for the past six months, they have not shared the same room. She told me the marriage was over, and they were just living together for the sake of their children. Sarah then told me that she could not find happiness with her husband, which has led to her excessive drinking at home and even using cocaine. She said that she was also working at a betting shop, despite knowing how it was negatively influencing her. She told me that she married her husband 15 years ago, not out of love but out of pity. Her husband is an African asylum seeker in England and was about to be deported back to his country, Sierra Leone, where a civil war was taking place. She married him so he could stay in the UK. However, despite being married to him for 15 years, she could not find happiness with him. Eventually, I found out that her husband was also an African asylum seeker like me. As the saying goes, 'Once you go black, you will never come back'.

Even after marrying her husband, the UK government did not cease their efforts to deport him back to Sierra Leone. The authorities believed that their marriage was fake. Sarah and her husband had to go through several humiliating, separate interviews at the UK Home Office, just to prove that their marriage was genuine. For instance, British immigration officers often asked Sarah questions such as 'When was the last time you had sex with your husband?', or 'Which position does he enjoy the most?'

Sarah said that she found the love and happiness she had been longing for all this time with me. I told her that it was impossible given that we have only known each other for a week. She said I was special. Later that day, I took Sarah to the room I lived in. My room was devoid of any possession. There was no TV, not even a bed—only a mattress on the floor. The room was actually a temporary place for me at that time, offered by two friends who heard that I was homeless.

Sarah made herself comfortable in my room, showing no sign of unease at all. When Sarah left that day, my conscience was weighed down with guilt because I did not tell her to stay with her husband or even try to sort things out. I did not tell her that happiness cannot be found outside of ourselves. Nobody and nothing can make us happy, and if it does, it will only be temporary. I did not tell her that we human beings are already finished, completely manufactured products built to achieve happiness within ourselves. We only need the body, the mind, and our breath to achieve happiness. Sarah was stressed out with her everyday life and looking for happiness outside of what she already had. She felt overjoyed being with me, but she did not know that what she was feeling was not true happiness at all but merely something transient.

One afternoon, two weeks after she visited my place, Sarah phoned me. With tears and her voice cracking over the line, she told me that her husband found out that she was seeing me. She asked if she could stay with me for a while, and I said yes. When Sarah arrived at my place, she was full of tears as she expressed how much she already missed her children. I listened to her intently without saying a word.

The next day, I told Sarah that I was not working. I could not offer her a place to stay because I could not afford the rent, and I had a week to vacate the room. Sarah agreed to pay the rent so that we could stay there together. I told Sarah that I really appreciated what she did for me, but the best solution for her was to go back home. I told her that I could not give her the happiness she was looking for. Even if she were with me, her whole life would not be any different at all. I asked Sarah to find contentment within herself, without any expectations from her husband—not even affection—and just to go home.

Sarah told me she could not possibly continue living with her husband. If she went home, she would only drink and take drugs. Moreover, she was also suffering from asthma and epilepsy. I asked Sarah if her husband was violent, had a bad attitude, and if he did not look after the family. She replied that her husband was a kind person who had a good job and looked after their family well. Her only complaint was that they had nothing in common. In my head, I could not understand why Sarah could not be happy at home—with a nice house, a husband, two beautiful children, and a job.

Her situation helped me gain a deeper understanding of one of the four noble truths stated by the Buddha. Human life is characterised by dissatisfaction and suffering. No one is exempted from dissatisfaction. Rich or poor, black or white, a local or an illegal immigrant, suffering is a characteristic of human life. Sarah's pain was so deep because it was not physical pain. She thought I was in greater pain because I had no place to stay, no job, and was nothing but a destitute asylum seeker. Even though she felt sorry for me at the time, I believe her pain was greater than mine. I agreed to stay with Sarah because I did not want her to carry on with her vices. I had to set her on the path to meditation and, similarly, Sarah did not want me to live on the streets. She believed she had to do something, and I felt the same way. It was a win-win situation for both of us.

Even though I was a destitute asylum seeker, had no place to stay, and, most of the time, had no food to eat, the pain I was going through was merely physical and superficial—the kind of pain that can be healed easily. Thus, I did not consider myself as someone who was suffering. I was simply somebody who had basic needs that could not be met. On the other hand, the kind of pain Sarah was going through was what I would call the deepest kind of pain. It is the kind of pain we all suffer from, no matter what kind of person we are. It is dissatisfaction. Sarah had everything to live for but could not find happiness at all. The only thing I could do for her was to propose a treatment, one that the Buddha had already proposed to all human beings.

First, I told Sarah that she suffers not because she could not find happiness with her husband but because she has not yet attained freedom. This is the kind of freedom in which we let go of all our attachments—the highest level of freedom. We have political freedom, economic freedom, and so on. All these are lower levels of freedom; the highest level is when we no longer live from the ego within our consciousness. This is why the Buddha stated that suffering comes from within, from all our attachments and desires. Nirvana, the end of suffering, comes from the abandonment of our desires and attachments.

Just from the second day Sarah spent with me, we started practising. In the morning and before going to bed, we would sit in meditation. During the day, Sarah and I practised walking meditation around the park, bringing nature back into her life. All that time, I continued advising Sarah to go back to her husband. I knew for a fact that she would not find happiness with me. I told her that now she was on the path to freedom, she should go back home and sort out her marriage.

I told Sarah that I was impermanent. I was merely a flux and a change that have temporally taken the form of a human being. She might see me today, but tomorrow may hold a different story. Therefore, she has to attain freedom. Still, Sarah did not want to leave me and return to her husband. She was concerned that if she left me, I would be homeless again; she was taking good care of me. Every time she came from work, she would bring me food to eat. Despite this, however, I told her not to worry about me and that I would be fine. She remained steadfast in her refusal to go home.

The guilt I was feeling with living with someone else's wife continued to fill my thoughts. I could not understand why I met Sarah and why she found me so special to the point that she refused to return to her family. What was more important to note was the fact that she no longer felt the need to drink or take drugs but has found relief in sitting in meditation. Each time Sarah would get upset over the urge to drink, I asked her to focus on her breathing, or we would do the walking meditation exercise. Through this, she dissipated the energy of her addiction. That was when I started contemplating on the question of why I got to meet Sarah.

While reading scriptures, I came across the following sentence: 'Let it come, let it be, and let it go'. And, for me, this was the answer to the question in my head. I understood everything. I had to let Sarah come and be with me. When she finally decides to go, I will have to let her go. I also understood that Sarah had a part to play in my destiny, if I had one. At that time, I could not really see it.

Sarah has had asthma and epilepsy since she was just 2 years old, a situation that has led her to take at least 20 tablets every day. Her breathing problem also required her to use inhalers all the time. Meditation helped Sarah greatly. We would count breaths and concentrate on our breathing, which played a vital role in stabilising her asthma. We would sometimes stop breathing repetitively, thus increasing the capacity of her lungs and helping decrease her asthma attacks. As meditation helps regulate and control the mind, it also helped Sarah stabilise her seizures. Anxiety and panic sometimes cause seizures. By meditating regularly, Sarah freed herself from anxiety and panic. Sarah even told me that her daughter, who was just 13 at the time, sits in meditation without anybody telling her to do so, all because she has seen its impact on her mother's life.

Just before I left the UK, I met Sarah's husband. He told me that he felt no hatred at all toward me, and that he really appreciated how I introduced meditation to Sarah. He pointed out the great improvement he saw in Sarah's life. I did not expect this kind of reaction from her husband. I misjudged him. Any normal person would have expected him to be mad at me for taking his wife away, yet he assured me that I was not the problem in their marriage. On the contrary, he blamed himself.

13
RETURNING TO LIVERPOOL

I fled from Liverpool because I no longer felt safe in the city where I openly spoke and protested against the killing of asylum seekers in the UK. I was receiving threats; the house I was staying at was set on fire. I was kept in a police cell and under police surveillance as well. Despite these things, I somehow found myself back in Liverpool a year later. I carried with me the same worry for the well-being of destitute asylum seekers. This time, however, their mental health was my main concern.

For destitute asylum seekers, the UK government is the reason why they cannot be happy with their lives. Before I started meditation, I shared the same view. However, because I am on the path to freedom, I have realised that this is not completely true. Achieving happiness in life is primarily our own responsibility—not of someone else, other institutions, or governments.

However, asylum seekers remain frustrated in the UK, as most of them are destitute with no food, home, and work permit. The difficulty they experience in their daily lives have led them to a maelstrom of sorts—some suffer from mental illness, explore prostitution, or become addicted to alcohol and drugs. In fact, some would become mentally ill because they refuse to accept the reality of their lives: their expectations and perceptions of the UK before they left their countries are not in tune with their actual experience.

We should also take note of the fact that some have spent huge amounts of money just to enter the UK, turning it into a kind of investment but without return. This is the main reason many asylum seekers would seek comfort in things like alcohol and drugs. As a destitute asylum seeker, I also took refuge in drugs in my pre-meditational life. Every single day, I smoked weed and cigarettes to escape the harsh, unbearable, and traumatising reality.

Meditation changed all that. It helped me break free from drugs and cigarettes. Meditation stimulated me mentally, enabling me to accept the harsh reality of a destitute asylum seeker in the UK and remain happy. I became compassionate toward destitute asylum seekers. It was then that I decided to share my experience with them, and introduce them to meditation in the hope of helping them cope better with their lives. To do this, I had to go back to what most people considered as the headquarters of asylum seekers—St. Anne Catholic Church's charity, Asylum Link, in Liverpool.

When I arrived at Asylum Link, asylum seekers were, as usual, complaining about their quality of life in the UK. In particular, there was a destitute asylum seeker from Angola—Denis—who was complaining to a charity worker named Janet. Janet works at Asylum Link as a cooking teacher, specifically teaching classes on how to cook English food. I could tell that Denis was furious as he was telling Janet that he will never be happy unless he was granted asylum in the UK. I intervened and told Denis that although we are part of a marginalised group, we can still be happy. Nothing can stop us from being happy if we really want it. He then asked me how we could be happy when we are destitute with nowhere to sleep, nothing to eat, and not even allowed to work? In response, I asked Denis to explain to me how some people who have food in abundance and live in mansions remain unhappy with their lives, to the point that they are driven to commit suicide. Denis couldn't find anything to say. I told him, 'You see, the problem is deeper than you think, and those you accuse of being the root of your unhappiness are not really the cause'.

Janet was delighted to hear me utter those words. She asked me what had happened as she knew me as someone who always used to point fingers and as someone who is heavily involved in social activism. I told her that I discovered a new way of thinking outside the box. Now, I'm learning to look inside myself, because deep within us is a huge universe brimming with treasures. Janet then asked if it would be possible for her to know what this way of thinking was that created such an enormous change in me. I told her about meditation. She was shocked. She said that she is actually a Zen Buddhist and that she has been practising meditation on a daily basis.

I told Janet that I was back in Liverpool with a proposal: teach meditation to destitute asylum seekers in addition to the material support that Asylum Link gives them. Janet was heavily pessimistic about this idea. For her, there were too many reasons that would prevent asylum seekers from understanding meditation. One, as most of them were either

Christian or Muslim, they might perceive meditation as another religion being prescribed to them, thus creating resistance.

In the end, I still decided to open a meditation class, and although doubtful, Janet agreed to assist me. I submitted an application to the charity to open a weekly meditation class for asylum seekers, and the charity administration invited me to discuss it. The administration was also reluctant because they wanted the charity to remain as secular as possible. I had to convince them that the practice of meditation has nothing to do with religion and is even scientifically proven.

Two weeks later, I started my first meditation class. I was surprised to find only one asylum seeker in the class, a person from Zimbabwe. The rest of the participants were all British citizens. Getting asylum seekers into meditation proved to be a highly demanding task. Despite the difficulties, I continued my efforts with the belief that this was what they needed the most. Here is the speech I gave at my opening class:

> *I would like to say thanks to all of you for being here. I really appreciate your time. I would also like to especially thank Asylum Link for its constant and renewed efforts to helping asylum seekers in any way possible. By allowing this meeting to take place in these premises, Asylum Link has shown its genuine desire for the well-being of asylum seekers, acknowledging the fact that the economy and politics are not enough for our well-being.*
>
> *Before saying anything concerning meditation, it is important to mention that, based on my experience, the practice of meditation has helped me greatly, and I am*

here to share the benefits of this practice with my fellow asylum seekers.

First of all, I would like to say that meditation has nothing to do with religion. If you are a Christian, you will remain a Christian; if you are a Muslim, you will remain a Muslim, and so on. There is no holy book of meditation. In meditation, we do not talk about God. To be specific, I should have said that the one that I will be proposing to you does not talk about God. When it comes to God, everyone has to decide for his or her own. So, don't worry. I am not trying to convert anybody. It is also important to mention that the practice of meditation is older than any religion you can think of. We cannot trace exactly where and when this practice started; however, the history of meditation is not important. What's important is how we, through meditation, can live a balanced and harmonious life, whoever and wherever we might be.

Now, what is meditation? And why should we practice it? Meditation is like water. We have been drinking water since our birth. Despite this, we still cannot say how water tastes like. Water is not tasteless. We just cannot define its taste. However, as soon as we drink it, we become familiar with its flavour. This is similar to meditation. Meditation has been defined in different ways such as to think of one thing continuously, to clear our mind, to truly know what we are, to see our true nature, to look inward, to be conscious of consciousness, to reflect on and be aware of ourselves, to regulate and control the mind, and so on. All these definitions are limited, and do not hit the mark. Having said this, I prefer to define meditation on this particular occasion as a practice that helps us regulate and control our mind. Why should we regulate and control our mind?

The answer to this question is: the battle of our lives is won and lost in our mind. The mind is the most important thing a human being can possess (if we can even possess it), and it is our single, most important duty to look after it. Anger, happiness, poverty, riches, sickness, life, and death—these are all derived from the mind. Two people might be in the same circumstances, but one can be happy, and the other may not feel the same way, and this says a lot. Thus, happiness doesn't depend on external factors. It only depends on our state of mind, and meditation helps us reach this state of mind. I presume happiness is what all of us live for. We go to work to pursue happiness. We travel the world and seek asylum for the quest of happiness. We even go to war for the quest of happiness. Yet, we don't seem to be happy. We are still faced with the same anxiety. In fact, some people in poor and conflict zones, such as Somalia, Sudan, and Afghanistan, are happier than those in England. Bhutan, which is a tiny and poor country in the Himalayas in Asia, has been ranked as the eighth happiest country in the world and the happiest country in Asia—happier than Japan, China, and Qatar. The country with the highest suicide rate is Japan despite it being one of the richest countries in the world. Therefore, happiness is just in our own mind. How to set it on the right channel by attaining the right understanding of life depends on our mind-set, and this is one of the benefits of a sustained meditation practice.

Scientifically, there is no doubt. Meditation has been proved to be a form of therapy. It reduces blood pressure, which is responsible for stress, anxiety, and tension. There is even a correlation between meditation and our brainwave patterns.

Spiritually, I will not talk too much about the benefits of meditation, because I don't want to be immaterial. I will just say that it helps us become more tolerant, compassionate, and patient. It has the power to change our lives, and it also clears all kinds of pain as meditation allows us to reach a state of freedom in which all the five conditions are absent, mainly sensation, conception, discrimination, awareness, and dualistic consciousness. Dissatisfaction and pain are just derived from these five conditions. We are aware that we are destitute asylum seekers, and this creates suffering. We are aware that we will die, and this, too, creates suffering. This goes on. However, awareness can also create pleasure. The same goes for sensation, conception, discrimination, and dualistic consciousness. Let's look at these three following events.

When Michael Jackson was doing a Pepsi advert on stage, something went wrong with the setup, causing his hair to catch fire while he was dancing. However, Michael did not immediately realize that his hair was on fire. He just carried on dancing as if nothing was going on. The staff had to intervene to stop the fire. What happened was that Michael was no longer in the realm of sensation and awareness. Michael was one with everything. Michael, the music, and the fire were one. Michael entered the state of freedom. In yoga, this state is called 'oneness' or 'Samadhi'.

The Pride of an African Migrant

The same thing happened to Berhane Selassie, commonly known as Bob Marley, in his concert in Zimbabwe in 1980. While performing, teargas was thrown on stage, and all the other musicians and Berhane's backup singers all fled, but Berhane remained unaware of what was happening around him. He just kept on dancing and singing without knowing that the music stopped. He could not even feel the effects of the teargas. He and the teargas were therefore one. Through the incident, he also entered a new realm. A realm of no sensation and no awareness.

My last example is of a Japanese surgeon. While conducting an operation, an earthquake occurred and all his staff members ran out. The surgeon, however, carried on with his operation. He was unaware of the earthquake and only knew about it when he was told about it later on.

What happened was that Michael and Berhane, through their music, entered the state of freedom—a state of no sensation and awareness. Because of being in that state, they could no longer feel pain. The same thing happens to us when we go to a hospital for an operation. They have to give us anaesthetics for us not to feel pain. Doctors have to make us enter the state of freedom, which is a realm of no sensation. However, it would be impossible for Michael and Berhane to have entered this state without their music. It is true that those who take huge amounts of drugs can enter this state, but those drugs have so many side effects in the long run, and these people end up in mental homes. However, the practice of meditation allows us to enter this state whenever we want with no side effects. Meditation is an anaesthetic. It has the power to dissolve pain. Those who have been practising it for a long time know that meditation is a refuge. Meditation is a real refuge, and it is where we should all seek asylum. We left our countries thinking that the United Kingdom would be a refuge, but here in the UK, we are destitute. Some of our fellow asylum seekers are being tortured while others are getting killed. Let's seek asylum in meditation, and we shall find refuge in it. Because in the state of freedom, there is no immigration, no asylum seeker, and no destitution. It is simply bliss. I want us asylum seekers to be like Michael Jackson and Berhane Selassie. To keep on dancing, singing, living, and enjoying life, through teargas or fire.

As I have said, the practice of meditation is done to regulate and control our mind. However, we cannot only expect to control our mind by sitting for half an hour in meditation. Meditation is everything we do in our daily lives. Let our lives become the expression of our meditation practice. Thus, I urge you to take this practice wholeheartedly, and you shall see its benefits. Pretty soon, you won't be annoyed with your immigration status.

After this speech, I was approached by the only asylum seeker present. She told me that she had been living in the UK for so many years and that all that time, she has been destitute. She said that she could barely sleep at night as she is mentally tortured. Every day, she prays to God that she be granted asylum. She also said that she and her friends had organised a prayer group with receiving asylum in the UK as their main intent.

After she finished talking, I said to her, 'I don't want to hurt your feelings, but what you're doing is adding more pain in your life. The more you pray to God to help you get your asylum in the United Kingdom, the more you suffer mentally. Because you become dependent. You increase your desires. You start waiting for something. But with the practice of meditation, I want you to get all of these things out of your head. Let go. I want you to be without desire, and you won't be mentally tortured. I am a destitute asylum seeker myself, like you, but I don't think of that anymore. I am no longer waiting for a stay, and I am even planning to return to my country. Will you waste all your life waiting for the UK government to grant you asylum for you to be happy? Enjoy this moment. You might even pass away without having those papers. I want you to enjoy life'.

In response, she told me that she had been trying to forget her condition, but she was simply unable to do so. She felt as if she were of no use in society and powerless to do anything. I said to her it is not easy to forget. In fact, it is almost impossible. The only time we can forget is when we sit in meditation, and even this takes so many years of sustained practice. The Chinese call this 'tso-wang', which means 'I sit and forget everything'.

As beginners, it is difficult to sit in meditation and start forgetting everything. What we should do, in this case, is not to pay attention. By refusing to pay attention, all those thoughts that mentally torture us will cease. I advise you to sit for 20 minutes in meditation in the morning and evening. Although the system does not allow you to work because of your status as a destitute asylum seeker, I would advise you to try your best to occupy your time—write, read, draw, play sports, engage in community work or voluntary service and so on.

I spoke to many African migrants who were granted a stay in the UK after years of struggle. I asked them if they were happy now that they were allowed to stay in the UK. Almost all of them said no. Some said they felt homesick, some expressed their desire to return to their countries, and some told me about their difficulty in landing a job. There were even a few who explained to me that they are married with children from women they do not love at all and that it all happened for the sake of being allowed to stay in the UK. They are not happy with their new home, and they have to share the same bed every night with women they felt no affection for.

All these migrants thought that being granted a stay in the UK would make them happy: a speculated answer to the unknown cause of their unhappiness. Now came the realisation that all those years of struggle, sleeping rough and enduring detention and torture proved to be worthless. As a result, some were already setting plans to return to their own countries.

Nevertheless, many Africans die just to enter Europe and those who already made it in Europe are fighting to stay legally, all under the belief that being where they are will bring them happiness. In the UK, asylum seekers and illegal migrants commit suicide in detention centres.

Unfortunately, I held my meditation class just for two months, and it was time for me to return to my country—to Cameroon.

The Pride of an African Migrant

PART 7:

PRIDE AND DIGNITY

The Pride of an African Migrant

14
RETURNING HOME

Africa is the continent of billions of possibilities–the main driving force behind international meetings such as the EU–Africa Summit, France–Africa Summit and US–Africa Leaders' Summit. The China–Africa Summit and Russia–Africa Summit are the latest ones on the list. With Africa as the heart of the world, these summits have their corporates in Africa—multinationals.

Africa has at least 60% of the world's natural resources, with almost 1.3 billion people, as well as millions of square miles of inhabited land. Every year, the economy of most African countries reaches a two-digit growth. In fact, the Portuguese government actually borrowed money from Angola, an African country. Moreover, the Portuguese are massively immigrating to Angola, and the Chinese are massively immigrating to many parts of Africa. Alongside this massive immigration, Africans are leaving Africa.

We cannot say that Africa is underdeveloped because of its lack of big industries, hospitals and roads. If we consider 'underdevelopment' in this sense, I can assure you that Africa would have been developed and can be developed within five years because the continent has everything. This includes enough qualified people, intellectuals and mineral resources to become a developed continent within five years.

However, what Africans lack greatly in are pride and dignity. The underdevelopment that Africa suffers from is a mental one, to the point that even the brightest of minds in the continent remain underdeveloped, as they lack pride and dignity.

This is the main reason why we can see African intellectuals working all their lives in Europe and America, contributing to the development of other parts of the world instead of their own continent. This opposes the statement Marcus Garvey once made:

> 'Education is the medium by which a people are prepared for the creation of their own particular civilization, and the advancement and glory of their own race.'

There are African doctors, bankers, scientists and even nuclear scientists devoting their lives to the development of Europe and America and forgetting their continent in the process.

The African continent is paying a high price for this immigration. Every year, thousands of Africans immigrate to Europe, causing a drastic reduction in the African workforce, of its valuable people and of its active population. This is one of the obstacles that Africa is facing on its road to development.

Even intellectuals in Africa who desire to go abroad are considered to have underdeveloped minds. In a sense, these

African intellectuals are like prostitutes—they neither have pride nor dignity, living only to fulfil their materialistic desires. It's similar to intellectuals who, when they are not selling their brains abroad, are selling it to dictators in Africa. In light of this, George B. N. Ayittey wrote the following for ECADF Ethiopian News:

> 'The most painful and treacherous aspect of Africa's descent into tyranny and economic decline has been the wilful and active collaboration by Africa's own intellectuals, many of whom are highly 'educated' with PhDs, and who should have known better. Yet a multitude of them sold of their conscience, integrity and principles to serve the dictates of barbarous regimes. As prostitutes, they partook of the plunder, misrule and repression of the African people. Some of their actions were brazen. In fact, according to Colonel Yohanna A. Madaki (rtd), when General Gowon drew up plans to return Nigeria to civil rule in 1970, 'academicians began to present well-researched papers pointing to the fact that military rule was the better preferred since the civilians had not learned any lessons sufficient enough to be entrusted with the governance of the country'.

The five years I spent in the UK awakened me to the realities of the life of an African migrant in such a place. A life characterised by homelessness, hunger, imprisonment, lack of pride, torture and assassination. The illusion of Europe as a paradise has totally vanished from my mind.

I phoned my family and told them that I was returning home. I was expecting my family to be happy about my return. However, they became upset with my decision, telling me that

England is the best place to be in. They went on, saying that there is only suffering in Africa and that there are no jobs. Most importantly, they told me that I was not welcome home. For my father, I was the stupidest person on Earth. For him, it was ludicrous for someone to leave a rich country like England to return to Africa. I was taken aback by my father's words and my relatives' cold treatment. However, it was not only my family who was not supportive of my plan. Even my friends in England did not want me to return home. Despite being irregular immigrants, homeless and destitute asylum seekers, they remain steadfast in their belief that England is a paradise and that happiness only exists in England.

What comes to my mind to describe this illusion in which my friends and relatives are in is the allegory of the cave that Socrates described to Plato's brother, Glaucon.

> *Socrates described to Glaucon a group of people who have lived their lives chained to a wall of a cave, compelled to stare at the blank wall in front of them. These people would watch the shadows of the figures cast by the fire behind them. They begin to ascribe forms to these shadows, and this served as their way to viewing reality.*
>
> *Socrates then supposed that a prisoner was released and permitted to stand up. If someone were to show to him the figures that made the shadows on the wall, he would not be able to identify them as they were, believing that the shadows on the wall are more real.*
>
> *Socrates then continued that if one of the prisoners was taken out of the cave, after some time, he would understand that the shadows he saw in the cave were not*

real and that whatever he was seeing was just based on his own projection.

With all these, Socrates asked this question: when this released prisoner goes back to the cave to tell the other prisoners that the images they see on the wall are not real but just their own projections, would he be killed by the other prisoners?

My friends and family—including myself—in particular, and most Africans, in general, represent the prisoners. Representing the prisoner who was taken out of the cave to experience reality is me. The shadows my friends and family see on the wall are their imaginations of England and their imaginations of a paradise outside themselves. They believe that there is a place where there is no suffering and where people live happily—England. However, for sages like Socrates, if such a place exists, surely it is in our own mind: the way we perceive and see things.

Irregular immigrants and destitute asylum seekers who sleep on the English streets also represent the prisoner who was taken out of the cave to experience reality. The difference is that they still refuse to accept that the images they saw on the walls of the cave—their perception of England before leaving their countries—were just their own projections and illusions. They cling onto that false idea of England in their minds, which is why they continue to suffer and sleep on the cold streets of England.

On May 2012, I presented myself voluntarily at Smithdown Lane Police Station in Liverpool. I handed my Cameroonian passport over and told the police that I wanted to be sent back to my country. I was asked to wait for immigration officers. Thirty minutes later, the officers arrived. They checked my passport and confirmed that I have indeed overstayed my visa. As a result, my asylum case was refused, and I absconded. Immediately, the immigration officers turned harshly on me, placed me in handcuffs and had me transferred to another police station. There, I was searched from top to bottom. All my clothes were removed from my suitcases and placed inside plastic bags. I was expecting to be treated with kindness; instead, I was dehumanised, treated like an animal just because I was an irregular immigrant who wanted to return to his country. I was locked up in a police cell for 48 hours. Then, I was transferred—handcuffed—to Pennine House, an immigration removal centre in Manchester, at around 4:00 a.m., together with other asylum seekers and immigrants. When we arrived, we were searched all over again. All our belongings were taken away from us. For immigrants caught on the streets, they were sent back to their countries without any of their belongings. Those who had homes were not even allowed to be escorted back to their places to collect their belongings. Many were deported with just the clothes that they were wearing. We were treated like dogs without any respect.

Immigrants at Pennine House were all in despair. They did not want to return to their countries. Many of them had already stayed in the UK for more than eight years; for them, there was no way they would return as they do not have the faintest idea where to start as soon as they were back in their home countries. However, for me, the starting point was in the mind, and this was the motto I used to encourage immigrants who were about to be sent back to their countries. I tried to get them to understand that their lives were not over, and that they were just moving from one place to another.

At the centre, the tension was increasing. Detainees were developing anti-white behaviours. Many were threatening violence against white people as soon as they were back in their countries. If we base this on the concept of cause-and-effect, some of these immigrants will go back to their countries and join terrorist groups and start kidnapping Westerners. It would be biased to label them as terrorists without considering the causes simply. When I returned to Cameroon, I saw many white people in the capital city of Yaoundé. I saw how they were treated kindly. I saw how Cameroonians would bow to them.

Seeing all that, all I could think about was how Africans are discriminated in the UK. For me, it was a disturbing scene.

In Pennine House, there was an art room where detainees could write notes. Before leaving the holding centre, I wrote a note to my fellow immigrants to dissipate the anti-white behaviour. This is what the note reads:

I wish we could all be like migratory birds. Free to move, travel around the world, live and settle wherever we want, without immigration control and border agencies. Our respective governments expend millions of dollars on anti-racism adverts on TV, while their policies remain discriminative. During my stay here in England, I met genuine people who want to make a change; however, they are powerless. They can only create an impact to such an extent. Whatever you do, I beg you; please do not hate white people. Do not hate British people. For the past few days, I was tempted to form racist views because of the way I have been treated. However, in the moments I think about this, I would think about the lovely white people I have come across with, and an energy of compassion arises within me. Please remember a white person who has shown kindness to you, and you will be fine. Happiness is not found in a particular place. You don't necessarily have to be in the United Kingdom for you to be happy. When two people are put in the same situation, it is possible for one to be happy and the other one to be unhappy. Therefore, there cannot be an index of happiness. Happiness is just a state of mind. You wrote this.

After writing this note, I was transferred to Campsfield House, an immigration detention centre in Oxfordshire. There were at least 200 immigration detainees in Campsfield. Unlike Pennine House, it was comparatively bigger. There was a gym, cinema, sports hall, library, church and mosque. The centre also had an art room where detainees could draw, write poems and display their works. Two weeks after arriving there, I decided to write poems and display them. However, my poems were perceived by the centre's administration as racist and inciting violence; they denied my right to display them. I thus decided to stick a note on my back that said, 'You denied me the right to speak because I am a nigger'. Detainees started asking me about the note on my back. Soon after that, I was knocked to the ground by at least 10 officers who said that I was trying to incite a rebellion inside the detention centre. Thus, I was placed under close surveillance. Later that day, I was visited by the detention centre's general manager. We discussed the basic rights of detainees and their right of speech. To give you a clearer picture, here are some of the poems I wrote.

POEM 1

I wish we could all be like migratory birds, free to move, travel, and settle wherever we want without immigration controls and border agencies. Why can't we learn from birds? They do not fight to feed themselves because they know the following truth: there is enough in this world for everyone's needs. Western governments expend millions of dollars on anti-racism adverts on TV, while their policies remain segregative and discriminative. Yesterday, you called me a 'nigger', and I protested. I thought I won, but today, you call me an illegal immigrant. How can I win this one?

POEM 2

You have the power to make this world a beautiful place, but don't you dare do so because it is beauty against justice. To live in a beautiful world is to hide and cover injustice. What would you prefer? Beauty or justice? To make this world beautiful is to live and dwell in a nondualistic world and to transcend good and bad, and right and wrong. However, to live in a dualistic world where every single thing, idea, and concept have its opposite is to suffer. May you live in the moment.

Detainees in Oxfordshire were all in despair. None of them wanted to return home; they were ready to go to extremes to stay in the UK, with some detainees even going on hunger strikes. When I arrived in Campsfied, I met a group of six Sudanese nationals who were on hunger strike in protest of their impending deportation. On my arrival, I was told that they had already been on a hunger strike for at least two weeks. As a result, their bodies were already very frail to the point that they could not walk on their own or even speak. These six people were then taken away from the centre. Until today, I still do not know where they were taken to. According to a detention officer I talked to, he revealed that these six Sudanese nationals were taken to a location where they would be force-fed.

Findings of a commissioned review of the UK government show 'people are being locked in unacceptable conditions in immigration detention centres.' However, some detainees were even happy to be locked in the detention centre than return to Africa. For instance, there was a Gambian detainee who used to tell detention officers that, being in that detention centre for him was just like being in a five-star hotel. He told them that they could detain him forever but he would never return to the Gambia. Because of this, 'Five-Star Hotel' became the nickname of this Gambian detainee. He was even happy to be called this way, but he never knew how stupid this made him look.

Having seen despair and dissatisfaction, I tried to lecture on happiness to my fellow detainees. I told them to focus on the mind, but they did not listen to me. I was taken for a fool. For them, happiness is to be in the UK—even if it means being locked up in detention centres. In this case, they rely on others to be happy, becoming slaves of the system. I remember something I used to tell ill-natured detention officers:

'You are making a fool out of yourself if you think that I'm in prison and you're not. In fact, I'll go back to my country very soon, and you will remain in this prison'.

They would reply:

'We have a choice to be here. You don't'.

My response:

'You think you have a choice, but if you look deeper into it, you don't. You are as helpless as those immigration detainees. You are here because you have to pay your mortgages. You have to pay your phone and TV bills, eat and buy clothing—where exactly are your options? We are fighting the same war. We have a common enemy: capitalism. So don't think you're my adversaries'.

For the UK government, most asylum seekers—if not all—are just economic migrants. There is no threat at all on the lives of asylum seekers, hindering them from returning to their countries. This is why the UK government labels them as 'bogus asylum seekers', a term that means fake asylum seekers. While it may be true that 80% of detainees are economic migrants, but the fact remains that there are asylum seekers who genuinely need the UK government's protection. For instance, there was a Jamaican asylum seeker in Campsfied who was deported back to his country. Two weeks later, he was assassinated.

I will not put all the blame on the UK government as it is a difficult task to determine who is a genuine asylum seeker and who is not, especially when it comes to those from corrupt countries. In these countries, people can produce fraudulent documents—fake arrest warrants, backdated newspapers and much more—with members of the government as their accomplice to support their asylum claims. For instance, to support their claim, a fake asylum seeker would present a fake arrest warrant signed by the chief of police and marked with all the necessary national stamps. In fact, this fake arrest warrant is not fake at all because it is delivered and signed by the right authority, albeit corrupt officers. Of course, it is fake in the sense that the government is not aware of this arrest warrant.

Some heads of states of corrupt countries who are incapable of governing their countries justly abandon their responsibilities by openly allowing their citizens to produce fake national documents to seek asylum in other people's countries. Such actions take advantage of the generosity of other countries. This is the case of the former president of the Democratic Republic of Congo (DRC), Mobutu Sese Seko: 'If you see that my country is hard, you can go to Belgium to seek asylum, use my name to say whatever you want if that can help you to get asylum'.

Now, what kinds of means does the UK government have to differentiate a fake asylum seeker from a genuine one when both present the same documents obtained from a corrupt country to support their asylum cases? However, whatever criteria used by the UK government to grant asylum, these criteria do not reflect reality. There are cases where the UK government grants asylum to fake asylum seekers and denies asylum to genuine ones.

I am not here to ask the UK government to grant all these people asylum. Instead, I am here to urge the UK government to put a system in which asylum seekers are treated fairly, either in being approved or rejected, in recognition of our shared humanity as contained in the New York Declaration for Refugees and Migrants adopted unanimously by the United Nations General Assembly on September 19, 2016. One of the commitments of the New York Declaration for Refugees and Migrants is to protect the safety, dignity and human rights and fundamental freedoms of all migrants, regardless of their migratory status, at all times.

Let me tell you the case of my friend, a Zimbabwean asylum seeker who goes by the name of Love More Zindoga. For several years now, Love More has been having problems with his kidney. Every week, he spends 72 hours attached to a machine in the hospital, just to clean his blood as his kidney can no longer do so. Despite his heavy reliance on drugs and machines to stay alive, the UK government refuses to cease all efforts in having him deported back to Zimbabwe where there is no hospital with adequate infrastructure. To persuade the UK government and prevent his deportation, doctors had to keep sending reports on Love More's health every three months to the UK Home Office.

The case of Love More is not only one of the many pieces of evidence that confirms the inhumanity of European governments claiming to be civilised, but also questions the real mission of the so-called Western humanitarian and non-governmental organisations in Africa.

However, the UK is not to blame if there is no adequate medical infrastructure in Africa. Africans simply have to blame themselves because they fail to value their dignity. During elections, they sell their votes. A banknote will surely get you a vote even if your platform would end up selling the whole country. Africans have to understand that money does not fall from trees. If a presidential candidate gives you money to vote for him, when they get elected, the money will simply return to their pockets out of the taxpayers' money—money that is supposed to be for building infrastructure.

It is stupid for African countries to say that they are independent when they have no adequate medical infrastructure. In fact, take a look at all those shameless African presidents who go to Europe and Asia for treatment when they are sick instead of building hospitals in their own countries.

After three weeks spent at Campsfied, I was given a ticket to return to Cameroon on June 14. I had to stop in Brussels then take a direct flight to Cameroon. On the due date, I was escorted to Heathrow Airport by immigration officers, and my passport was given to the pilot. After a 45-minute flight, I arrived in Brussels around 9:45 a.m., where the Belgian police were waiting for me. As soon as I got off the plane, I was handcuffed and taken to a cell. I displayed resistance at the airport as I refused to be handcuffed—I was not a criminal. I was voluntarily returning to my country. However, they treated me brutally. I was asked to remove all my clothes and left naked in a cell. Under such circumstances, I refused to board the plane to Cameroon. At around 6:00 p.m., I was taken back to England by plane—handcuffed just like a terrorist. Everybody on the plane was looking at me. They were all frustrated and scared. For me, that flight was a brutal one. I could not help but let the tears run down my face.

However, those tears were not tears brought about by weakness. I did not consider them as my tears alone. They were the tears of all black people since slavery, forced labour and colonisation were brought upon us. Those tears were asking the same question Bob Marley asked: 'Could you be love and be loved? Don't let them fool you'. At that moment, I thought of Jimmy Mubenga. I tried to imagine how his last moments were: 'I can't breathe', said Mubenga, minutes before the angels of death of the UK Home Office took his life. His last moments were in tears, but those tears were not tears brought about by weakness; rather, they were tears of victory—a victory of barbarism over humanity, hatred over compassion: They were tears of humanity.

I did not want to experience Mubenga's last moments. So, I surrendered to the UK Home Office. Around 7:00 p.m., I arrived back at Heathrow Airport in London. I was then transferred to the Colnbrook Immigration Removal Centre, a former prison turned detention centre. Here, we were locked up in our cells 23 hours a day. We were not allowed contact with anyone. The toilets were located in the cells themselves, and there were cameras everywhere. After three days in Colnbrook, I was transferred back to Campsfield. I spent another three weeks there before being given another ticket to return to my country on July 4. This time, I was escorted to Cameroon by good-natured immigration officers. I actually enjoyed the flight. It felt great to return to my country.

Mama Africa
...Long time me no see you Mama... In you there's so much beauty. In you there's so much life. In you there's so many kingdoms... You're the maker of gold Mama. You're the maker of diamond. You're the maker of pearls.
And the maker of all precious goals... You're my mother Africa. You're my father Africa. I'm proud of you Mama. I love you Mama. I'm proud of you Mama. I love you heavenly...
—Peter Tosh

The Pride of an African Migrant

15
LET US KEEP OUR PRIDE AND DIGNITY

> 'The degree of people's alienation is like
> those who wander into foreign lands
> forgetting their family and inheritance
> and live as destitute, preoccupied with
> scratching a living'
>
> —Dogen Zenji

From an outsider's point of view, observing Africans preferring imprisonment, torture and death over returning to Africa, people can hastily conclude that there must be a sense of pride in being an African migrant in Europe. As a returnee, I wrote this book with the sole aim to tell my African brothers and sisters the opposite: there is no pride in being an African migrant in Europe. The only pride is when we decide to return home, even with empty pockets. We need to stop celebrating when family members and friends go to Europe and America.

In their desire to escape from Africa, Africans have become cowards. Ironically, they consider crossing the dreadful sea to enter Europe as an act of courage. However, let me tell you that returning home empty-handed is the real sign of courage. Most African immigrants say that they cannot return to Africa because basic needs, such as electricity and running water, are not guaranteed. However, who is more courageous? The person who leaves Africa, or the person who stays in the continent? Without a doubt, it is the person who chooses to stay.

Although this book demands justice for African migrants in the UK, however, I did not only write it to condemn the country for its violation of human rights. But also to ask us Africans to stop being a disgrace to ourselves, to our continent and, most importantly, to our ancestors who fought with all their might, sacrificing their own lives just to preserve the dignity we now give away so easily.

On the coasts of Italy, African migrants agreed to be filmed naked by Italian immigration officers, because of their desire to enter Europe. The video made headlines in the global media, and Africans are accusing the Italian immigration of inhumanity. While I do not disagree, this incident is proof that Africans themselves are also to blame as they give away their dignity so easily—a dignity their ancestors have sacrificed their lives to preserve.

A French journalist once said that 'the life of undocumented immigrants is a life of a dog'. This journalist is right when people look at it from a lifestyle perspective. We sleep on the streets, steal, sell drugs and sell our bodies to survive. Is this the life people want to live? 'Open your eyes and look within, are you satisfied with the life you're living? We know where we're going… We know where we're from', said Bob Marley.

We become robbers, drug dealers, prostitutes and the mentally ill. As one of our great heroes of independence, Sékou Touré, always said, is it not better to return to our home countries and live in poverty with dignity and sanity rather than stay in Europe and live this kind of life?

There was this young African girl who sought asylum in the UK but to no avail. She had nowhere to live, no food to eat and no right to work. She told me that she had no choice but to sell her body to survive the harsh streets of the UK. She slept with different men in exchange for a roof over her head. As if this was not enough, upon the men's discovery of her status as an undocumented immigrant, they start getting violent against her. She had to face all of it because she had nowhere to go. When one man decides that he was done with her, she would be kicked out and left to find another man, and the cycle continues.

Is it not a life of dogs as the French journalist said? That young African girl told me that she had no choice, but how could she not have a choice? She had a choice. She can choose to return to Africa, instead of living a life of dogs. I met hundreds of undocumented African immigrants in the same situation. I even know some who have contracted HIV, became single mothers and had children without knowing who the father is. In fact, I even got to know a young African man who had to appear to people as homosexual just to stay legally in the UK. However, these are the questions that we have to ask ourselves:

(1) Is the legal stay worth all of this?
(2) Will the legal stay cure people from HIV or AIDS?

(3) After a man performs homosexual acts against his will, will the legal stay get rid of the pain he had to go through?

When you visit immigration centres in the UK, you can see old African women- our dear mothers, queuing up every day, begging for a stay. What would catch your attention, however, is the way our dear mothers are treated by young British immigration officers. British people do not share the same high regard that we in Africa have for the elderly.

I have a Togolese friend who came to the UK with all his children. One day, one of his daughters—just 13 years old at the time—started posting nude pictures on social media. Each time her father tried to talk to her, she would always say that it is her life to live. In the end, she reported her father to her teacher, who called social services for child abuse. When the social services turned up, they took the girl away from her father because they are in a world where everyone is equal to everyone. I do not blame the social services in this case. I only blame my friend. He put the education of his child at stake just for a legal stay in the UK. His daughter was brainwashed and alienated. She learnt the so-called human rights in the UK: the right to post nude pictures on social media and forgot the decency learnt from her African culture. In well-known Senegalese author Cheikh Hamidou Kane's prize-winning novel *'Ambiguous Adventure'* about the interactions of Western and African cultures, he asks:

> *Would what they would learn be worth as much as what they would forget? I should like to ask you: can one learn this without forgetting that, and is what one learns worth what one forgets?*

The Western world is the exporter of decadence. African children are growing up in this kind of environment—an environment that is morally and spiritually bankrupt just for the sake of the legal stay. They talk without respect to their parents; they dress as they please and they do what they want. 'It is not good to stay in a white man country too long', said the well-known Jamaican Rastafari dub poet, Mutabaruka, in his poem 'White Man Country'.

We have to keep our pride and dignity. We have to emancipate ourselves from the psychological bondage of inferiority and destroy the European myth. We have to shed the shackles of the past. Marcus Garvey wrote:

> 'The time has come for the Blackman to forget and cast behind him his hero worship and adoration of other races, and to start out immediately to create... Then why not see good and perfection in ourselves?... They have sprung from the same family tree of obscurity as we have; their history is as rude in its primitiveness as ours, their ancestors ran wild and naked, lived in caves and in branches of trees like monkeys as ours; they made sacrifices, ate the flesh of their own dead and the raw meat of wild beasts for centuries... Who can tell what tomorrow will bring forth? We see and have changes every day; so plan, work, be steadfast and do not be dismayed... Let no religious scruples, no political machination divides us, but let us hold together under all climates and in every country; making among ourselves a RACIAL EMPIRE upon which, the Sun shall never set... NATURE first made us what we are and then out of our own creative genius we make ourselves what we want to be. Follow always that great law. Let the SKY be your

limit, and Eternity our Measurement. There's no height to which we cannot climb by using the active intelligence of our own mind. Mind creates, and as much as we desire in NATURE, we can have through the creation of our own minds...'

'Each generation must, out of relative obscurity, discover its mission, fulfil it or betray it', said revolutionary and philosopher Frantz Fanon.

'Each generation has pyramids to build', said African scholar Joseph Ki-Zerbo.

With this, the choice of whether we keep betraying Africa or we awaken now and achieve freedom is in our own hands.

16
WE CAN ACHIEVE OUR DREAMS WHILE BEING IN AFRICA

I know we immigrate because we want to escape from unemployment as well as the outrageous poverty and misery we are subjected to in Africa. However, when it comes to unemployment, Africa is not the only failure. There are unemployed people everywhere in the world. We can achieve our dreams while being in Africa.

In the modern version of Wallace D. Wattles The Science of Getting Rich, Sean Rasmusean's The Law of Attraction it is stated: In The Road to Universal Wealth, 'getting rich is not primarily a matter of environment'.

Thus, we do not have to risk our lives, waste all our savings, leave our families, take loans and go on a crazy adventure to Europe for the quest of wealth. By doing such, it is probable that we will simply be adding more misery into our lives. As mentioned, it is important to remember that the creation of wealth is not primarily a matter of environment. Qatar, for example, was formed on a desert landscape. In terms of its environment, nothing has really changed.

However, the people in Qatar did not stop there. To create wealth, they had to create it themselves. They did not consider moving to the US or the UK as options. Instead, they created wealth in their desert by asking themselves what the desert can offer. Now, their desert has been transformed into cities. They managed to build one of the world's tallest buildings there. They created Qatar gas in their desert. They created Al Jazeera television in their desert. They created Aspire Academy and a Qatari foundation, planted trees and much more. Qatar was able to achieve this level of development despite the lack of diversity in its resources compared to those of African countries. Qatar mainly has gas and oil. Thus, it is not primarily a matter of environment.

> *'This tiny island of Cuba, without natural resources and placed in embargo by Western countries for many decades, has succeeded to achieve what no one has achieved elsewhere. In all these conditions, the government of Cuba has succeeded to guarantee free health care and education to all his populations. This Cuban success has always been the envy of African-Americans to whom they still inject syphilis or aids and are used for experimentations in the pharmaceutics market.'*
>
> — Prof. Michel Koumou, *Le Panafricanisme: de la Crise à la Renaissance.*

I know a young Cameroonian girl named Aisya. She was born in North Cameroon. At the age of 18, she moved to the Cameroonian capital city of Yaoundé. There, she learned sewing for two years. At the age of 20, she got a job as a domestic worker, and her salary was just USD 60 a month. Aisya was saving USD 40 a month out of her salary, and the remaining USD 20 went to rent for a small room. After a year, she managed to save USD 480. With this money, she bought a sewing machine. While working as a house helper, she also opened her own tailoring shop in the small room she was renting. After finishing her duty as a domestic worker, she would go home and started sewing robes and shirts. Business was booming as she started receiving orders from clients. The next year, Aisya was no longer saving USD 40 a month. She was now saving USD 80 a month. After a year, she managed to save USD 960.

Aisya was born in north Cameroon where most villagers rear cattle, so with the USD 960 that she saved, she went to the north and bought two cows. Farmers in the north who did not have their own cows were renting Aisya's cows to help them on their farm. While she was in the capital, her parents in the north were looking after the cows. They would send Aisya fresh milk from the cows to sell in the capital. Every year, each cow gave birth to at least three to four calves. Because she started with two cows, she was having at least six to eight new cows a year. The following year, Aisya was no longer saving USD 80 a month. She was now saving USD 200 a month, and she quit her job as a domestic worker. At the end of that year, she managed to save USD 2,400. With this money, she bought five more cows. She kept on selling cow's milk, having her cows up for rent and sewing. The following year, Aisya was no longer saving USD 200 a month but was now saving USD 300 a month. At the end of that year, she managed to save USD 3,600. With this money, she bought land for her cows. The following year, Aisya was now saving USD 400 a month. At the end of that year, she managed to save USD 4,800. With this money, Aisya opened a butcher's shop and a shop in the capital.

The Pride of an African Migrant

All these achievements within just five years! Aisya is now financially free. It is important to mention that she never went to school and only learned to speak French when she moved to the capital.

I had the privilege to meet Aisya and asked her if I could write her success story in this book to encourage others, and she gladly accepted. I also asked her about the key to her success. She told me that it was four things: determination, sacrifice, patience and humility. Aisya is a self-made woman. She started with just USD 60 a month, and she made it. She did not have to go to Europe to get success. In fact, I asked her if she had any plans to go to Europe one day. She only replied that she does not know anybody there and does not have any plan on what to do once she gets there. However, she was still open on the idea of going there should she have business partners in Europe in the future.

Today, any bank and microfinance in Cameroon would not hesitate to lend Aisya money if she really needs it because she has proven her reliability. How many immigrants in Europe can achieve what Aisya has achieved? When I returned from England, I did not even have a penny in my pocket. I could not even afford a taxi from the airport to my house after having spent five years in England.

I have met an undocumented Congolese immigrant in England. He has been in Europe for more than 20 years. Despite being deported back to Congo four times, he managed to come back to Europe each time with a fake ID. He told me that each time he entered Europe, he would spend at least USD 8,000. If we multiply that amount by 4, the total would be USD 32,000. This is a huge amount that has been put to waste.

Even in Europe, there are only a few locals who have this amount of money as only a few of them can save up to that degree. The last time I saw this Congolese man was in Liverpool, and he appeared to have become mentally ill. He could not recognise me at all. The sad thing is that I was not surprised at all to see him in this condition. I have met many immigrants who suffered the same fate.

We still have an inferiority complex toward Europe. This is the only way I can understand my Congolese friend's stupidity, which cost him his sanity in the end. However, he is not alone in this foolishness. Some immigrants spend up to USD 10,000 just to buy marriage and get to stay in the UK—not even a guarantee in the first place.

We Africans waste thousands and thousands of US dollars to go to Europe. It is a gamble. It is just like the lottery. What is the guarantee? Using that kind of money, one can open a small business in Africa with high potential for growth. It is also possible that in 5 to 10 years with the business, you would be able to afford vacations to Europe. This is so much better than wasting the money you have right now just to live on the streets of Europe, to be held in detention centres for years and be deported back handcuffed as criminals stripped off of all dignity. Making that bet is a waste of money and time. Africans spend at least USD 7,000, on average, to enter Europe. They end up just sleeping on the streets, selling their bodies, marrying men and women they do not love, selling drugs, being detained and being deported.

More than anything else, how can poor Africans afford to migrate to Europe? Even by taking the road through the desert or by sea, African migrants still need to have a reasonable amount of money that those who are considered poor in Africa cannot afford. 'Just to take a boat to cross the water to the Italian island costs USD 2,000', said a clandestine African migrant. Those who are poor in Africa live with less than a dollar a day. How can they afford USD 2,000? We can, therefore, say that poor Africans do not migrate—only the average Africans and the rich ones do so.

Poverty and misery are not the only causes. We can paraphrase the well-known Cameroonian philosopher, E. Njoh-Mouelle, and to some extent call this poverty and misery a false problem. In his book *'De la Mediocrité à l'Excellence'*, he wrote:

> *Misery in underdeveloped countries is not rigorously a synonym of hunger... We might have wondered if we are Africans by reading or by hearing declarations that underdeveloped countries are countries where people die of hunger. It is not certainly the African from rural areas who dies from hunger. We misjudge when we rely on calculations based on yearly income estimated in American dollars! The African rural man is someone who has something to eat every day, even if it is indefinitely the same menu every day. He lives from his farm's products, cultivated maybe without methods and particular research but offering crops that are more or less fertile. He consumes its banana, cassava... How can we say that he dies from hunger? And it is also not the unemployed African from modern cities who might die from hunger. For this to happen, he needs to have no cousin or uncle or any other relative having a job, which is unthinkable. In Douala, Abidjan or Lagos, we always have a well-situated cousin from whom we can take our*

meals and sleep at night. Neither the African family nor the sense of solidarity that unites its members is dead... We do not deny that man of the underdeveloped Africa experiences a certain misery. We precisely deny the idea that this misery resides in the fact of dying of hunger or not to eat as much as we want... The African of the rural areas who is no longer satisfied to produce for his or her own subsistence but now aspires to produce a surplus to go and sell in the city, in return, to buy clothes, forks and bread, he or she will only be miserable when he or she will experience the anguish of the aspiration never satisfied. Now appears the first form of misery that we call subjective misery, a painful awakening from the man... who separates his or her actual being from what he or she wants to be. The unemployed who seeks a job in the city goes through the same anguish. He or she doesn't have what he or she wants. He or she wants a job that is a guarantee of a daily bread. This misery resides in the consciousness of difference and distance. Difference between those who have and those who have not. Distance between what one does not have and what one will love to have. This misery is not specific to people of under-developed countries. People of developed countries experience the same anguish... Up to the extent to alienate our existence for an object, for a situation which is an object, a situation from the other side of a barrier that hypnotizes us through the force of the value of life that we have projected. What makes the subjective misery painful it is the servitude in which it puts us face to face with our aspiration. This misery is subjective because its cause can be judged unnecessary by others.

The Pride of an African Migrant

17
ESCAPISM IS NOT THE SOLUTION

Africans also immigrate because they believe that in Africa, they do not uphold the human rights they deserve. From my personal experience as a migrant in the UK, I have observed that in most cases, it brings more suffering than fulfilment.

Wherever we go, human rights are violated, and you have most probably experienced this first-hand in a foreign land against your expectations.

I recently watched on TV a documentary on Eritrean refugees in Israel who fled their country because of the lack of human rights. They fled thinking that in Israel, their lives would be better and their human rights would not be breached like in Eritrea. These Eritrean refugees walked through the Sinai desert to get to Israel, wherein many of them lost their lives and were buried in the desert. However, these Eritrean refugees also experience human rights violations in Israel. They have been kept in detention centres for years and years; those who were 'free' had no right to work, no home and no welfare benefits. They sleep on the streets of Tel Aviv, discriminated, and constantly victimised through racial assaults. According to the Ministry of Interior in the State of Israel, 'African immigrants are a threat to Israel's national security'. Consequently, the government of Israel is even building one of the biggest—if not the biggest—detention centre in the world near the Sinai desert, which will have the capacity of holding 1,600 asylum seekers at a time.

In addition, black Ethiopian Jews who thought that they were marginalised in Ethiopia immigrated to Israel in droves. However, they even face greater marginalisation in Israel. In her article 'The Hypocrisy of a Black Miss Israel', Ruby Hamad wrote:

> *Sadly, for most of these 120,000 immigrants [black Ethiopian Jews], it is a fairy tale that does not have a happy ending. Since the 1980s, Israel's Ethiopian community has found itself the target of both opportunistic and systematic discrimination.*
>
> *Living in highly segregated communities, they have complained of being refused jobs, housing and their children being denied places in school. This widespread and ongoing prejudice finally prompted thousands to protest on anti-racism rallies last year.*
>
> *But nothing signifies the endemic discrimination against this community more than the bombshell that was the Israeli government's admission that it was guilty of giving a birth control drug to Ethiopian Jewish women, without their full consent.*
>
> *While they were still in transit camps in Ethiopia, women were either misled or coerced into accepting injections of Depo-Provera. 'They told us they are inoculation', one*

victim told the Israeli investigative journalist who broke the story. 'They told us people who frequently give birth suffer. We look it every three months. We said we didn't want to'. While some were persuaded to have the injection, others were told, point-blank, that they could not immigrate if they refused the injections.

The birth rate of Israel's Ethiopian community has decreased by 50 per cent, with rights groups directly blaming the government's deliberate drive to forcibly restrict and limit the fertility of Ethiopian women.

Therefore, we have to come to the realisation that true refuge cannot be sought outwardly but only inwardly. Escapism is not the solution to our problems. We have to face and deal with them. It is said that he who runs away leaves the fight for another day.

The Pride of an African Migrant

PART 8:

GLOBALISATION

The Pride of an African Migrant

18
GLOBAL VILLAGE

Africans attempting to realize globalisation for themselves have become, in the process, the living sacrifice on the altar of globalisation—migration. However, globalisation offers great opportunities only with strong and powerful governments. For instance, OECD member countries with 19% of the global population have 71% of the worldwide trade in goods and services and 58% of foreign direct investment.

In this age of globalisation, will the British government be able to control the influx of migrants in the UK? Even if the British government were to use the most barbaric methods, they would not be able to stop it. Because one of the characteristics of globalisation is that 'it intensifies our dependence on each other, as flows of trade, investment, finance, migration and culture increase... I wish we could slow this globalisation train down, I told Adeeb, but there is no one in control' (Thomas L. Friedman, The Lexus and the Olive Tree: Understanding Globalization).

Mass migration is one of the consequences of globalisation, and globalisation cannot be stopped. This failure to cease, according to Lester R. Brown and Brian Halweil, is because no one is in control. If this is the case, how can we put a stop to this migration? We are condemned to live together.

'[globalisation] can breed in people a powerful sense that their lives are now controlled by forces they cannot see or touch. The globalisation system is still too new for too many people, and involves too much change for too many people for them to have confidence that even the good job they have will always be there. And this creates a lot of room for backlash demagogues with simplistic solutions. It also creates a powerful feeling in some people that we need to slow this world down, put back some walls or sand in the gears...' (Thomas L. Friedman, 'The Lexus and the Olive Tree: Understanding Globalization).

'Patriotism is a backward idea, inopportune and harmful... As a sentiment, patriotism is an evil and harmful sentiment; as a doctrine, it is nonsensical since it is clear that if every people and every state take itself for the best of peoples and states, then they have all made an outlandish and harmful mistake'.

—Leo Tolstoy

19
PROS AND CONS OF IMMIGRATION

Asylum seekers and immigrants in the UK have both positive and negative impacts. Every year, billions of US dollars are transferred from Europe to Africa. At the time of writing, African migrants sent USD 60 billion in remittance in the previous year alone. According to the World Bank, on average, migrants sending money home to Africa lose 12% to fees. Most importantly, they contribute to the economy of their host countries by paying taxes.

On one side, there are those who have been granted asylum and get to stay in the UK, creating wealth for the country. Meanwhile, there are those who hoist the British flag at the highest and bring more glory to the UK by winning gold medals in the Olympic Games and other major sports competitions. For instance, Mohamed Farah, a Somali refugee in the UK and a long-distance runner, has given the UK four Olympic gold medals and five gold medals in the World Athletic Championship, making him the most decorated athlete in British athletics history.

Just after France's victory at the 2018 FIFA World Cup, Venezuela's president Nicolas Maduro said during an official event in Caracas, aired on state television VTV:

'The French team won, although it looks like an African team. Actually, Africa won; the African immigrants who arrived in France. I hope Europe receives that message. Much they have despised Africa. They have looted it, enslaved Africans for 500 years, and in the World Cup, France won the trophy thanks to African players or the sons of Africans. Hopefully, France and Europe will appreciate that us, southerners, Africans [and] Latin Americans, are worthy and powerful. No more racism in Europe against African people, no more discrimination against immigrants'.

In fact, immigration has been widely shown to have many positive effects. For example, economists have found that crime is significantly lower in the English and Welsh neighbourhoods in the United Kingdom, with the largest immigrant inflows and that immigration raises local property values in Spain and the United States.

If you ask entry-level economics students what they would expect a large influx of low-skilled immigrants to do to the economic prospects of natives, most will reason that the increase in the labour supply will reduce wages and increase unemployment, perhaps especially for poorer, less-educated locals. But professional economists have found something very different: study after study has shown that opening up labour markets to more people has not only increased the supply of labour but also raised the return on capital investments, accelerated economic growth and thus increased the demand for labour—improving the lives of natives as well as those of the immigrants... One also has to accept that natives actually receive a greater economic gain from immigration than do the immigrants themselves.

On May 29, 2013, British immigration officers raided the Alternative Tuck Shop, a café just down the road from Oxford University's economics department, where South Asian and Middle Eastern employees serve tea, scones and sandwiches. The agents seized two young men, one from Bangladesh and one from Algeria, under suspicion of working in the United Kingdom without authorisation. And they shuttered the business temporarily, meaning that hungry Oxford economists would have to walk farther down Holywell Street for their midday panini.

Soon, the young sandwich-makers incarcerated and then deported from Collier's doorstep would have arrived in Algeria and Bangladesh, if they have not already. Some of the effects of their removal have been proved by stacks of economic studies; others are hypothetical. What research shows is that the economic value of those men's labour will decline by 60 to 80 per cent or more, reducing the size of the world economy; the job prospects of British workers will be essentially unaffected, given how little interest they have in low-wage service work; the British government will collect less tax revenue; Collier and his colleagues will pay slightly more for tea and cakes; and Algeria and Bangladesh will lose whatever money those men may have been sending home... Yet Collier [1] describes governments' putting forcible limits on immigration, to the United States and elsewhere, as acts of 'compassion'. This is a strange type

---

[1] Paul Collier is the author of *Exodus: How Immigration Is Changing Our World.*

of compassion, involving armed agents turning away desperately poor immigrants and deporting them if they somehow slip in.

Nor are governments providing charity to immigrants... In a 2013 study of 27 countries, the Organization for Economic Cooperation and Development (OECD) found that immigrants contribute an average of USD 4,400 more per household to the government than they receive in benefits each year. For 20 of these countries, immigrants' net fiscal contribution was positive; in the United States, that figure was around USD 11,000 per immigrant household. These numbers should not come as a surprise, since immigrants tend to be younger than natives, and most of them move to work, not to qualify for benefits. Their age alone means that they will work longer (thus paying more in taxes) than natives and will remain healthy longer (thus receiving less in benefits)

—Michael Clemens and Justin Sandefur, excerpts from *Let the People Go: The Problem with Strict Migration Limits*

To some extent, given the opportunity, asylum seekers and immigrants are arguably more likely to appreciate being given a chance to earn an honest wage. Some attend the kind of university that they could not have attended if they were still in Africa; others get jobs in Europe that are simply not available in Africa. In turn, this gives them the chance to enjoy luxuries—for example, chocolates made with cocoa beans straight from their own countries—which they may not have been able to afford when living on an African salary.

PART 9:

DEVELOPMENT

The Pride of an African Migrant

20
RETHINKING DEVELOPMENT

'I say, send them [refugees] to us we will accept them. They are all human beings. They can always come here. I will welcome them until we are filled to the brim'.

—Rodrigo Duterte, President of the Republic of the Philippines

The Philippines is evidence that there is no demographic, economic and social reason a country cannot open its doors to refugees. This country challenges and nullifies all reasons and excuses for not saving the lives of people in danger.

The Philippines is the 12th most populated country in the world with more than 120 million inhabitants within an area of 298,192 km² and a population density of 343 per km².[2] Demographically speaking, it is almost impossible for them to host refugees. However, the Philippines overcame its demographic challenge by welcoming thousands of refugees on her soil.

---

[2] As of the time of writing. According to the Worldometers, the Philippines ranked 12th from 2005 to 2016.

Unlike the Philippines, Australia is vastly underpopulated and almost uninhabited. Its population is 24 million for an area of 7,692,000 km^2 with a population density of 3.1 km^2.[3] Clearly speaking, Australia is an empty country that refuses to welcome refugees, preferring to live with kangaroos than fellow human beings. Australia deports those who are already inside the country, regardless of the UN multilateral treaty, the Convention Relating to the Status of Refugees or the 1951 Refugee Convention, signed and ratified by the Australian government.

According to the survey of the Social Weather Stations, a social research institution in the Philippines, 9.1 million Filipinos remain unemployed.[4] Refugees would need to find work for their integration, but the survey is evidence that the Philippines do not possess sufficient capacity to provide such need.

Despite the challenge in finding employment, the Filipino government welcomes asylum seekers and issues them work permits, giving them the right to compete against Filipinos for the few jobs available in the country. It's a situation comparable to how a poor mother of 10, who does not have enough to feed her own children, would still choose to share what little she has with other refugees. This kind of action challenges human logic and goes beyond ordinary human capacity.

---

[3] As of the time of writing (2016).

[4] As of the time of writing. The 2019 Third Quarter report of the Social Weather Stations states that the number is at 10 million.

The UK only has 4% of its population unemployed.[5] Nevertheless, asylum seekers are destitute in the UK and have no right to employment. Moreover, the UK government blames its unemployment on migrants. As a result, refugees are deported, tortured and even killed.

Walking through the streets of Manila, I saw an overpopulated society. I also saw the challenges and difficulties that Filipinos have to face and go through every day. Despite these challenges, the Philippine government abides by the 1951 Refugee Convention and its 1967 Protocol.

The Philippines has a long history of welcoming refugees. In fact, it has become part of the country's culture at least since 1940. The Philippines signed and ratified all conventions relating to refugees and stateless persons. Throughout its history, Philippine presidents have been in favour of refugees; they did not only welcome them, but also championed their rights. In 1940, then-President Manuel Quezon took in Jewish refugees. Former President Benigno Aquino III mentioned that, 'Following the Vietnam war, 400,000 Indochinese refugees that the Philippines accepted for temporary placement had, 15 years on, neglected to leave their "temporary" home and had become permanent residents'.

While Western countries continue to build walls, current Philippine president, Rodrigo Duterte, has offered to welcome the world's refugees until his country is full to the brim. In an interview with Al Jazeera, he asserted, 'I say, send them to us, and we will accept them. They are all human beings. They can

---

[5] As of the time of writing. The December 2019 update of the UK Office for National Statistics states that the rate is currently 3.8%.

always come here. I will welcome them until we are filled to the brim'.

This humanist statement from President Duterte is evidence that, in championing the rights of refugees, he has walked the extra mile than his predecessors and millions of extra miles than world leaders.

The Philippine government teaches a lesson on humanity: no one is too poor to give, and there is neither excuse nor reason not to save human life. The Philippines is an example that invalidates the excuses other countries give to deport, torture, imprison or kill refugees.

Another sad reality is that, if our world is full of refugees, it is mainly because of the external imperialist policies of countries like the UK, France, the USA and Israel. These countries are the ones that manufacture civil wars, sponsor terrorist organisations, invade other countries, overthrow legitimate and democratic governments and install dictatorship but are not willing to welcome refugees, leaving countries like the Philippines to clean up their mess. The former president of Zimbabwe, Robert Mugabe, shared the same view in his address to the United Nations' General Assembly on September 28, 2015:

> *The growing list of phenomena that neither respects nor knows any borders makes it imperative that we mobilise all mechanisms of co-operation to effectively overcome them… For some months now, we have watched heart-breaking and harrowing scenes of desperate refugees seeking to enter Europe in search of safety and shelter from the ravages of conflicts in their own homelands. We*

have also read of the tragedy and loss of life in the Mediterranean. The majority of the affected people are from Syria or from other countries devastated by conflict and instability induced, in great part, by the destabilisation policies of external forces. This tragic situation could have been avoided through respect of the independence of other countries and non-interference in their internal affairs. In the case of Libya, we are witnessing the results of abusing the authority of the United Nations Security Council and ignoring the opinion of regional organisations, in this instance, the African Union (AU), which are supposed to be the United Nations' partners in the maintenance of international peace and security.

This also raises the question of development and underdevelopment. What is development? By which standard a country is developed or underdeveloped?

Can Australia, Great Britain, France and the US still be called developed countries while they deport, imprison, torture and kill refugees? If yes, then what we mean by development is purely and simply economic. It is simply just numbers.

Can the US still be called a developed country while it kills millions of people across the world and massacres its African population daily? If yes, then what we call development is purely and simply power.

Can we still call the Philippines an underdeveloped or a developing country even though it opens its doors to refugees and protects them? If yes, then what we call underdevelopment is just the development of morality, humanity and love.

Development is highly complex. Each time we mention the word 'development', we should specify what kind of development is being talked about, whether it is economic, material, nuclear, moral, spiritual, human or others.

PART 10:

DENOUEMENT

The Pride of an African Migrant

21
WE ARE ONE

It is my hope that throughout this book, you have come to the conclusion that the Pride of an African Migrant is not only the pride of one person or of Africans in general; rather it is the pride of humanity in the sense that it defends the universal values of freedom, human dignity and justice. Since time immemorial, these values have always been the ideal that human beings desire to attain, regardless of their ethnicity, race, or religion.

For millennia, human beings have migrated, settling new lands, building empires or searching for work and new opportunities. This will stop neither today nor tomorrow. We live in a dynamic world—not in a static one. Everything is moving including planets. Some continents are actually moving closer to others, while others are moving away from each other. In science, this movement of continents is called plate tectonics. Nothing can remain static. Therefore, to be against migration is to be against nature. The well-known Ethiopian poet, Lemn Sissay, shares a similar view of migration in one of his works:

Birth is migration from the womb to the open air.
We are all immigrants.
Death is migration of breath and air.
The last migration. The vast migration.
Migration is our nature.
I have been sent to tell you.
Echo location. Echo location.
To be anti-migration is to be anti-nature.

—*EchoLocation. Echolocation. Echolocation*

In no way does this book intend to prevent Africans from going to the Western world. Its goal is to make Africans aspiring to migrate to the European Union or the US be more informed of the issues related to their plans so that they can be better prepared.

In the final analysis, mankind is just one. We all have a common ancestor that we, the Basaa people, call Hilolombi (the most ancient of ancients). We all come from the same source of life that we, the Basaa people, call Mbog.

It has been scientifically proved that Europeans and non-Africans, in general, are just Africans who left the African continent at a certain period in history. According to the father of African contemporary history, Cheikh Anta Diop, the skin colour of Africans who immigrated to Europe turned to that of Caucasians (whites) today because of the extreme cold back then, which lasted for many centuries.

Even the Chinese who, for so long, denied their African origin have finally agreed that their ancestors were blacks and Africans after the DNA tests of Jin Li, a leading Chinese geneticist and professor at the National Human Genome Center and Fudan's Institute of Genetics and also the vice-president of Fudan University, were released.

However, Prof. Jin Li started the project intending to prove the exact opposite. Responding to the BBC after the result of intense laboratory tests on hundreds of specimens came back, he said, 'We did not see any—even one single individual that can be considered as a descendant of the Homo erectus in China. Rather, everybody was a descendant of our ancestors from Africa'.

All those physical and psychological borders are simply illusions borne out of ignorance and egocentric desires. However, there are some that still firmly hold onto those illusions to the extent that they humiliate, torture and even kill others to defend their beliefs. Thus, it was with the sole aim to regain the honour, pride and dignity of the humiliated and tortured ones that this book had no other choice than also abide by such illusions. It is in the same light that Karen Mingst and Jack Snyder wrote in 'Essential Readings in World Politics': 'If the desire for power cannot be abolished everywhere in the world, those who might be cured would simply fall victims to the power of others'. Diop echoes the same sentiment:

> *'The planetary unification does not seem to be for today, whatever a superficial spirit can think of. At the moment, social consciousness is far from being taught to the world enough for certain obscure sentiments to be eradicated. Vigilance always remains the rule... The sincere fraternisation of people and planetary unification will be achievable from the moment when different people will equally be strong and educated, to the point that no one*

will imagine of cheating the other. Thus, the existence of continental states risks itself to be the prelude to the planetary unification.'

Universality and oneness of all beings are a reality, and their separation is just an illusion—this is what I strongly believe in. However, as long as the whole world does not walk at the same pace toward that universality for their own pride and dignity, each and everyone would have no choice but go along these illusions, whether they be racial or ethnic. Thus, this raises philosophical and religious questions such as 'Is it because others do bad things that I, too, should do the same?' We can even go further and ask ourselves, 'Is there really "good" and "bad" in the first place?' It is up to you to answer them.

People fight and countries go to war for a number of complex reasons, but their objective is the same: to reach a better position than before the conflict, ultimately for what they believe will be a happier life. However, history has taught us that well-intentioned conflicts often—or even always—result in disaster.

I would like to take this opportunity to thank Kenyan president, Uhuru Kenyatta, and his government for recognizing the Asian community in Kenya as the 44th indigenous group of the country. This action needs to be praised—whether it has political motivations or not, and whether we like President Uhuru Kenyatta or not—and must be cited as an example to follow. Therefore, I call upon the government of Myanmar and Indonesia to follow the Kenyan government by recognizing the Rohingya and Papuans, respectively, and to stop persecuting them. I also call upon the

Vatican and the Cameroonian government to recognize the right of the Basaa people of Cameroon, to stop the genocide of their heritage and culture as well as to stop persecuting all those who stand against this genocide.

Let us bring to realization the deep desire of humankind in Zen philosopher Shin'ichi Hisamatsu's *'Vow of Mankind'* for his students:

> *'Keeping calm and composed, let us awaken to our true Self, become fully compassionate humans, make full use of our gifts according to our respective missions in life; discern the agony both individual and social and its source, recognize the right direction in which history should proceed, and join hands as brothers and sisters without distinction of race, nation, or class. Let us, with compassion, vow to bring to realization humankind's deep desire for self-emancipation and construct a world in which everyone can truly and fully live.'*

The Pride of an African Migrant